LESTER PIGGOTT

Return to the Saddle

The definitive account of one of racing's
most extraordinary comebacks

LESTER PIGGOTT
Return to the Saddle

The definitive account of one of racing's
most extraordinary comebacks

by
Michael Tanner

Foreword by Brough Scott

EBURY PRESS
LONDON

First published in 1996 by Ebury Press

1 3 5 7 9 10 8 6 4 2

Copyright © Michael Tanner 1996

Ebury Press
Random House, 20 Vauxhall Bridge Road,
London SW1V 2SA

Random House Australia (Pty) Limited
20 Alfred Street, Milsons Point, Sydney
New South Wales 2061, Australia

Random House New Zealand Limited
18 Poland Road, Glenfield
Auckland 10, New Zealand

Random House South Africa (Pty) Limited
PO Box 2263, Rosebank 2121, South Africa

Random House UK Limited Reg. No. 954009

A CIP catalogue record for this book
is available from the British Library

ISBN: 0 09 185182 3

Edited by Coral Walker
Designed by Roger Walker/Graham Harmer

Printed and bound in Great Britain by
BPC Hazells Ltd, Aylesbury, Bucks

Papers used by Ebury Press are natural, recyclable products
made from wood grown in sustainable forests.

CONTENTS

Author's Note

This book was conceived the instant Lester Piggott announced his intention to make a return to the saddle. What Turf historian worth his or her salt could resist the opportunity to consign something to posterity on the subject of Britain's outstanding sports personality of the post war era? And, make no mistake, that is the only cap to fit Lester Piggott: a man who, for almost half a century, bestrode his sporting domain like no other Briton.

My sole aim was to produce a detailed and accurate chronicle of Lester's second coming, a definitive account of the riding comeback – however long it lasted. The alpha to omega; no more, no less. Mind you, where Lester is concerned, who knows when the game is over. Within two months of officially 'retiring' his name was linked with a celebrity race at Gosforth Park in Johannesburg. As it happened, the race eventually fell through, but he still climbed back into the saddle in order to join Willie Carson and John Reid for an 'exhibition gallop' during the opening meeting of a new racetrack at Siracusa in Sicily on November 8th 1995. Even as I write, Lester continues to assist his local trainers by riding out on Newmarket Heath of a morning. One such was son-in-law William Haggas, who, shortly before April's supplemental deadline for the Derby, legged him up on to the twice-raced Shaamit and asked whether the inexperienced and not yet race-fit colt had the action and balance to handle Epsom's notorious combination of turns, cambers and gradients: 'That's the sort of thing that a jockey has to feel and father-in-law knows a bit about what is required.' Lester gave the thumbs-up: Shammit went to Epsom and won the Derby. 'It's unbelievable', said the old maestro. 'It feels like riding a tenth Derby winner for me.'

It was not my intention to place the Piggott persona under the microscope in an attempt to discover what makes the man tick. One must accept that prising open the rustiest pot of paint is child's play compared to lift-

vii

ing the lid on the psyche of Lester Piggott. Plenty of would–be Freuds have tried and failed on that score. Even the two books written with Piggott's active co–operation have disappointed many readers. Of *Lester: the Official Biography*, written by Dick Francis and published in 1986, the *Sporting Life* reviewer was reduced to saying: 'You cannot put a genie in a bottle or a book'; and nine years later the sport's other trade paper, the *Racing Post*, in its review of *Lester: the Autobiography* , confessed to 'a constant niggling irritant he should have shared more with us'.

In trawling for the necessary detail to compile as accurate a picture as possible, I have cast a wide net; any material of highly specific origin is duly acknowledged. But I should like to extend particular thanks to James Fry at the International Racing Bureau, photographers Trevor Jones and John Crofts, Cherry Forbes and Sue Connolly at the *Racing Post* and, not least of all, that paper's Australian correspondent, Jack Elliott.

Michael Tanner
Sleaford
July, 1996

FOREWORD

This book needed writing. And it needed Michael Tanner to write it.

For Lester Piggott's comeback was so much the stuff of fairytale that much of the coverage was away with the fairies too. Such an approach does not do justice to the achievement of what will remain one of the most unbelievable sporting accomplishments in this century or any other.

Now Lester has finally quit the racing saddle, you wonder if it really happened. Did we really have that October afternoon at Belmont when Dayjur jumped the shadow? When two horses perished in the sprint? When the super filly Go for Wand hobbled horribly on snapped stumps of legs in front of the stands? And when Lester saved the day by sweeping through on Royal Academy in the Breeders' Cup Mile to land the richest prize of his whole professional life just twelve days in from a five year come-back? It couldn't have happened but it did.

When Lester flashed past with all that old inevitability intact, I remember the ghostly chill of seeing the past come to life. It was the most unreal thing I have experienced in 40 years studying the madness of the racing game. As always Lester had stepped right into the eye of the storm. Like many others I had had my doubts at the wisdom of his return, but in that one ride he threw a bridge across the unhappiness and scandal of the years away. He had returned to state that he was the greatest jockey ever to bestride the turf and it was on that turf that his career would close.

And exactly two years later it looked as if he had gone out on his sword. The Breeders' Cup Sprint at Gulfstream, Mr Brooks going down before the turn, Lester Piggott a still and bloodied figure with the oxygen mask across his face. I remember pulling myself together to try and find the words for death in the afternoon. By some miracle these worst fears proved groundless and there were two more seasons for the last embers of that supernatural talent to burn away.

But just because Lester Piggott inspires such memories, evokes so much emotion, so too is it important that a writer with a cool historian's hand should put this final riding chapter into a sensible perspective. Michael Tanner is that writer. Read this and you will see that he has done his work well.

Brough Scott

PROLOGUE

They never come back. From boxing to tennis; from football to...racing: they never come back. So runs one of sport's oldest and most recycled canards. They might not, but 'He' did. Like Muhammad Ali, his alter ego of the ring, Lester Keith Piggott had rewritten enough rules in his time to recognise this one was no more binding than the rest.

Lester: not many sportsmen, and certainly precious few jockeys, are ever readily identifiable by christian name alone. Exactly what is responsible for this public acclamation defies adequate definition. Boy Wonder? There have been plenty of those. Punters' Pal? Ditto. Mr Nice Guy? Hardly. The Anti-Hero? Getting warmer, perhaps. Piggott cut a mysterious figure, a man of few words who let his actions speak for him. He'd steal mounts from other jockeys, steal races from under their noses and, on one infamous occasion, even steal a rival's whip ("I only borrowed it") in order to ride a finish after he'd lost his own. Old-fashioned heroes don't do these things. Lancelot, Beau Geste or Biggles would rather die than stoop to such subterfuge. Piggott, on the other hand, acted out his equestrian version of *My Way*: he made his own rules, usually as he went along: that way the rules could be broken whenever it was deemed expedient. Piggott was the archetypal maverick: essentially law-abiding but with hints of a ruthlessness we'd rather not know too much about; a man not to everyone's liking but revered nonetheless.

Reaction to the 'Second Coming' of Lester Piggott was understandably ambivalent. Joe Public could anticipate even the dullest day's racing being enlivened by the presence of the Maestro; the return of the 'house-wives' choice' made the drawing pin redundant in a million homes come Derby day, whilst simultaneously striking fear into the hardened hearts of bookmakers throughout the land. Young Turks like Dettori, Weaver, Munro and Holland, who had come to the fore during Piggott's sabbatical, looked forward eagerly to the opportunity of pitting their wits against Old Stoneface. Who, one wondered, would first dare utter 'Move over Grandad' and reprise Piggott's own alleged mid-race orders to Gordon Richards and Scobie Breasley back in the 1950s when he originally burst on to the scene.

Some, however, were openly sceptical. Surely the old bones would soon creak and cry out for a rocking-chair instead of a saddle. Among the doubters was Willie Carson, one of Piggott's many arch rivals from the glory years. Five years was a long time to be away from the hurly-burly of raceriding, he said. 'We don't want Lester to seem a shadow of his former self. Lester was a real legend and we don't want the memory to fade.'

Despite Carson's misgivings the racing canvas was to be enriched for five more years by the broad, glorious strokes of the master. Royal Academy's irresistible surge to the wire in the Breeders' Cup Mile just 12 days after the comeback began; the power-packed, iron-fisted drives which saw Mudaffar and You Know The Rules grab the spoils at Doncaster in 1991; the velvet-gloved finesse displayed on Lord Carnarvon's two fillies, Niche and Lemon Souffle; and, perhaps above all, the consummate manner in which Rodrigo de Triano was nursed to four Group I victories in 1992 that included the 30th English Classic. Any one of these highlights justified the comeback. And Piggott's own personal highlight? His answer says it all: 'The highlight of the comeback was.... to come back.'

1

TURNING POINT

When Oscar Wilde ventured to suggest that 'Prison life makes one see people and things as they really are', he was naturally referring to his own unhappy ordeal in Wandsworth and Reading gaols, but the sentiment could just as easily describe the outcome of Lester Piggott's 12 months inside Highpoint. Society's sending him to prison, according to Wilde, ranked with his father's sending him to Oxford as a turning point in his life. However, whereas prison broke Wilde and arguably drove him to an early grave at the age of 46, a mere three years after his release, Piggott's detention at Her Majesty's pleasure arguably resulted in more positive repercussions. Anyone who has come into contact with Piggott since his release on October 24th, 1988 – and there have been more in the subsequent eight years of Piggott's life than the previous 52 – testify to the unlikely phoenix which has risen triumphantly from those unpromising ashes.

Willie Carson, for one, is adamant: 'One thing coming back to riding has done is bring the smile back to his face. He'd forgotten how to laugh and life seemed to have drained from him; but the old twinkle is back now. And that can only be a good thing.' The late Charles St George, for whom Piggott rode umpteen winners down the years, observed in 1992: 'After coming out of prison Lester was like a man who has been through a serious illness. He was far more relaxed and never worried about anything, even money. He is very relaxed these days and happy with life generally. It was in the retirement years that he was unhappy. He was so very bored. Frankly, he only had one hobby and that was riding horses. Now he is riding again he is enjoying life. He is at peace when he is in the saddle.' Another confidant of long-standing to notice a change is Peter O'Sullevan: 'Lester is a complex, private person. Since his year in prison he has been a changed man, to his enormous credit – much more communicative and articulate. He is more sensitive to other people's feel-

1

ings. Before, he never thought about anybody else, was utterly ruthless about nicking the best ride. When he came out he was talking about the disaster of the prison service, the iniquity of incarcerating people who weren't criminals when they went in but were sure to be when they came out.'

Although Susan Piggott maintained that her husband came out of prison the same kind of man who went in, her daughters did notice a difference. Maureen echoed St George's view: her father had become more easy-going, enjoyed his success for what it was, and was genuinely touched by the public's affectionate response to his comeback. Tracy Piggott was even more effusive: 'He's a better person for having been in jail – more open and relaxed, more laid-back, more jolly. Being in prison made him realise the importance of doing what you want to do. I think he decided, "Right, I don't particularly like training, and when I get out of here I'm going to do what I want, which is to ride horses." I've never thought of dad as shy. He can be outgoing and funny. But there's a certain reserve about him and when he was younger a dedication to his sport that required a lot of concentration. These days he has less on his mind. He's easier to talk to. He hasn't come out of it bitter or angry.' She continued: 'Nowadays people can't understand why he's called Stoneface because he never stops smiling. And he's riding again not because he has to but because he wants to. He is enjoying himself so much since he returned to the saddle. There's not so much pressure and he's doing it purely for the fun. He's become a happier man. He's doing things now he never used to do, like personal appearances and opening betting shops.'

Indeed, Piggott's face hardly ever seemed not to be smiling out from a picture of some promotional event or another. Two months into the comeback he opened a new George Atkins' betting shop in the centre of Nottingham: it was the very first time Piggott had consented to such an undertaking. He dutifully autographed 200 colour photographs and looked more than happy to do so. He also co-operated in a TV commercial for Cadbury's Creme Eggs. A specially-made £3,000 version of his latex *Spitting Image* puppet was commissioned for the advert, which depicted him riding a vigorous finish on a creme egg. 'I like to go for the inside', he confides while attacking the egg's filling.

From latex to Cutex. The nail polish manufacturer launched a 'Create-A-Plate' project to raise money for the Arthritis and Rheumatism Council for Research. Various celebrities from stage, screen and sport – Richard Gere, Ryan Giggs, Lennox Lewis, Linford Christie – were supplied with a selection of nail polishes, a white plate, chinagraph pencil and ceramic

The elder statesman of the Flat joins some of Newmarket's senior citizens as they prepare to embark on their annual day trip to Yarmouth *(Vernon Place/Racing Post)*

pen, and asked for a contribution that could be auctioned. Seventy plates were returned, including Piggott's which bore his signature above a horse and jockey framed by a horseshoe. Another manifestation of the new, more mellow Piggott was captured by Lord Lichfield in a photographic portrait of Lester with his young grand-daughter Mary-Ann Haggas, one of twelve celebrity pairings picked for the work 'Generations of Kodak' which promoted the company's new photo CD system. A further photo opportunity availed itself on the occasion of the annual day trip to Yarmouth, for over one thousand of Newmarket's senior citizens, sponsored by Bill Gredley. There it was once again: a beaming Lester Piggott, so obviously in love with life, surrounded by adoring members of the public.

This generosity of spirit did not square with Piggott's legendary meanness, a legend bolstered – and distorted to monstrous proportions – by literally hundreds of anecdotes, some true, most apocryphal, that had been seized upon and recounted time and time again over the preceding 40 years. That a penny-pinching streak did inhabit the Piggott psyche was

3

undeniable and, for that matter, it still does. For instance, on the flight home from one of his numerous European sorties during the comeback, Piggott gleefully accepted the courtesy mini-bottles of champagne though he had no intention of imbibing them on the plane: each one went into his hold-all for later consumption. What he did not realise was that whilst he made an in-flight trip to the washroom his thirsty jockey travelling companions extricated the bottles and replaced them with their own empties. Piggott would enjoy the joke, for much of the poker-faced, skinflint legend is contrived.

In truth, Piggott revels in this notoriety, courts it, and rarely misses an opportunity to play up the parsimonious image for all he is worth. He does buy the petrol sometimes when sharing a car to the races and he has been known to buy the ice creams. But as the reporter opines at the end of John Ford's classic Western *The Man Who Shot Liberty Valance*: 'When the legend becomes fact print the legend'. And yet it is worth asking, for example, whether the following exchange could have transpired in the old days before Highpoint. At a Windsor evening fixture in June 1993, a German racegoer called Hanna Smart approached Piggott as he walked out to ride Barahin in the Montrose Selling Stakes. 'Lester, I need a winner!', she implored. 'Has he got a chance?' In years past one could guarantee such an intrusion would have gone totally unheard, tactically misheard or quite possibly even received short shrift. Not so now. Piggott mumbled: 'Good chance'; and duly got the 7–2 shot home by three-quarters of a length in a pulsating finish.

What can be stated without fear of contradiction is that racegoers around the world flocked to see him wherever he pitched his tent. In this regard the legendary Piggott factor had not altered one iota. The trend set by the first day at Leicester – double the crowd and betting shop turnover up by £3 million – soon became commonplace. If anything, the reincarnated Piggott was bigger box office than the original. The best part of 1,000 people jammed Racecall's switchboard to hear the commentary on his comeback ride at Leicester. Old fans were overjoyed to receive this unexpected gift of another chance to pay homage to 'a national treasure' or 'the great antiquity' as he was quickly dubbed; and they were eager to blood the young and uninitiated while the offer still existed.

Barely a month of the comeback had elapsed before Piggott was merrily undertaking a punishing schedule round Europe which encompassed visits to Saint-Cloud, Evry, Livorno, Milan, Marseilles, Madrid, Dusseldorf, Milan again, Rome, Maisons-Laffitte and back to Saint-Cloud within the space of two weeks. By the conclusion of the Second Coming in March 1995 Piggott had ridden in two dozen different countries stretching across five continents.

Everywhere the reception was the same: complete idolatry. For the official opening of the Jebel Ali track in Dubai, Lester was sponsored in aid of a local charity. Everyone who bought a ticket was entitled to meet the great man at the house of trainer Dhruba Selvaratnam. As all the back-slapping adulation began to pale, the Piggott brain turned to mischief. To ease the monotony he would now and again open the door of Selvaratnam's office and release Rocky, a fiesty Highland Terrier who disliked strangers. 'Lester kept sidling over to open the door and letting out the dog, who made its presence felt and hurried visitors along', recalled the trainer. 'It was very funny and typical of Lester. Eventually the room was cleared, but only after Lester had kept letting the dog out!' And when he turned up in the Slovakian capital of Bratislavia for the first time, the local organiser Marian Surda said: 'This will present Slovak racing to the world.' The winter tour of the Far East proved an annual moneyspinner for all concerned. There was not a ticket to be had for the 1991 Indian Derby at Bombay's Mahalakshmi racecourse once Piggott's participation was announced; trainer Patrick Biancone only ran Mastermind in the 1991 Hong Kong Derby to give Piggott a ride in the race: 'I do not think a world-class jockey like Lester should be sitting in the stands when a race like this is being run. I am convinced that if Mastermind is to have a chance it will only be because Piggott is riding him.' In Ireland he was a veritable Pied Piper. From Ballinrobe and Killarney (new attendance records at both) to Tralee (2,000 extra on the gate and Tote turnover up 40 per cent) his drawing power in the land of the horse was stronger than ever.

Back home we witnessed the revival of that perennial question 'What will Lester ride in the Derby', complete with its customary many and varied answers. Hokusai proved the solution to the 1991 conundrum but not before Piggott's name, in time-honoured fashion, had been linked with no fewer than nine other horses. Hokusai never looked a potential tenth Derby winner. Nevertheless, Piggott's presence in the saddle caused bookmakers to halve his odds of 66–1. Coral's Wally Pyrah defended the move with the priceless words: 'If Lester rode a donkey in the Derby we'd have to shorten its price!'; his Ladbroke's counterpart Mike Dillon agreed: 'We didn't miss Lester when he was away but now he's back we realise what tremendous appeal he has. He's got a great following and some people will only bet on him.' If Hokusai had defied logic and won the 1991 Derby the bookmakers' coffers would have been £15 to £20 million lighter.

Besides the annual pre-Derby Piggott puzzle, the traditional brushes with authority and his wonderful knack of putting noses out of joint remained fully operational and provided plenty of newspaper copy. The very first ride at Leicester resulted in a stewards' enquiry and it was not long before he incurred the first suspension: four days from the Saint-Cloud stewards on December 4th, 1990, for 'making insufficient effort' on Lady Isis.

Then, in 1991, he aided and abetted Barney Curley in the latter's personal crusade against the major bookmaking firms, which involved withholding information about the riding arrangements for the horses belonging to the Newmarket trainer and gambler. In the morning papers of August 7th Curley's Threshfield had no jockey for Pontefract's Jim Gundill Memorial Handicap. Arriving racegoers, however, were greeted by the tannoy announcement 'In the fourth race Threshfield will be ridden by L. Piggott', and the buzz that went round the course was soon translated into money. Threshfield was backed from 11–8 to 11–10 and Piggott duly did the business, getting the 5YO home by a rapidly diminishing head. 'I did not book Lester until this morning because he is due to ride in the seven o'clock at Kempton and I was not sure if he could get here', Curley informed the press angelically. 'But I have no qualms about not having a jockey up in the papers: all it does is mark the cards for the bookmakers for their early morning betting sham. This is in protest at the money taken out of the sport by the Government and Britain's big bookmakers... one way to change the Government's attitude is to cause enough trouble to make them take notice.' Three weeks later, the mischief-makers struck again. Piggott had been booked to ride horses for Simon Dow and Brian Gubby at Nottingham but instead he turned up at Kempton to partner Threshfield. 'Lester rang me yesterday to say that he was going to Kempton and that was perfectly all right by me', said Gubby. 'It's typical Lester, though, isn't it?' Threshfield was beaten a neck and a head into third.

In early May of 1993 it seemed Lester had once again been spotted cocking a snook in the direction of the punters' best interests: on successive days at Lingfield Park he appeared to commit the jockey's cardinal sin of 'dropping his hands' toward the finish, an act of folly costing his mounts their best possible placing and, more to the point, one which caused thousands of betting slips to be torn up in offices all around the country. On Friday, May 7th, he rode the 3–1 shot Young Ern in the McCall Group Conditions Stakes and conceded defeat very quickly when Winged Victory raced up to him, and then past him, along the rails; 24

Reunited with old allies, Henry Cecil and Charles St George *(Trevor Jones)*

hours later, Able Choice, his mount in the William Hill Rated Stakes, who had been backed down from a morning line price of 6–1 to 7–2 favourite, was palpably eased in the final 75 yards and lost third place on the post. Just to compound the issue, Saturday's race went out live on BBC Grandstand. Nevertheless, apart from John McCririck, who pointed an accusing finger at a 'toadying media intent on hushing up widespread public concern', nothing was said in the press and no action was taken.

Both instances did seem bad errors of judgement on Lester's part, albeit in the case of Young Ern's race made to look worse by the camera angle – a point made by Piggott when reviewing the incidents with Julian Wilson during the BBC's Newbury coverage the following Friday (the day McCririck's article appeared): I did put my hands down in the last five or six yards on Young Ern. Looking at the TV, it was a bad angle and people probably thought it was closer than it was. The winner was flying at the finish and I wasn't going any faster. He was going away from me. In the other race everything went wrong that could have gone wrong. The horse is bad in the gate and he went in last but the starter couldn't let them go straight away because another horse started playing up. My horse went forward two or three times to get out and I dropped my whip. Then I got squeezed out between the first two. It probably didn't look as if I was doing much but the horse couldn't have gone any faster.' Repeated viewing of the video confirmed Lester's account of each race, and in Able

Choice's race, suggested – as Wilson did – that a whip might have been useful in the fight for the third place. 'A big help', replied Lester with a rueful chuckle.

A further opportunity to pillory Lester for ostensibly disregarding the interests of others surfaced in the summer of 1994. Malmo's Jagersro Racing Club thought it had Piggott booked for its Swedish Derby meeting; his picture was placed on the cover of the racecard and £15,000 spent on advertising the publicity coup. Piggott subsequently told them he did not feel up to riding after a recent spill; the day of the race saw him riding the Queen's Sharp Prod in Berlin. 'I'm afraid this means the end of Lester Piggott and the Swedish Derby', said Club Secretary Benny Karlsson. 'He has tried to play too many cards.' Before the month was out, however, Piggott was back in Sweden, riding at Taby in Stockholm. As always, the Piggott factor overcame all obstacles and slights.

Another European disappointed with Piggott's attitude was the German owner Arnold Nothdurft, who contracted the jockey to ride all his horses during 1992; the arrangement lasted four months. Even an Irish owner, Pat O'Kelly, for whom Piggott had won the valuable Group III Prix de Psyche at Deauville aboard Danse Royal, ultimately decided she could stand no more and took him off the filly. 'Lester is so difficult. He is always so on and off. He rode a lovely race to win the Prix de Psyche but in the Meld Stakes at the Curragh last time he got shut in. He then annoyed me by saying that the filly did not try. It is difficult to try when you are in a pocket. You cannot talk to Lester. At least we know his replacement will do what we ask of him.' For once the biter was well and truly bitten. Seldom, however, did Piggott come unstuck. 'When he rode his last winner for me at Baden-Baden I told him to make the running', recalled trainer Peter Walwyn. 'He jumped out, made all the running and won. Great jockeys like Lester don't need instructions.'

Getting on the good horses remained the paramount consideration. A booking for the Barry Hills-trained Surrealist in a Listed race at Doncaster in September 1991, for example, was instantly ditched in favour of the last-minute opportunity to partner Arc candidate In The Groove in her Goodwood prep race. One or two people smiled after the filly was beaten and Surrealist won; and Piggott did not get the ride in the Arc, either.

Piggott's singular attitude, though well documented – when there was public clamour for a knighthood upon his retirement Paul Haigh, of the *Racing Post*, suggested it should be 'For services to Lester Piggott' – was rarely condemned. In the wake of the 'Malmo Affair', however, *Sporting Life* columnist David Ashforth dared confront the issue. In a piece entitled

'Taking hero worship too far' he wrote: 'Piggott's behaviour was repre-hensible yet some people's reaction will be one of sneaking admiration because what is viewed as inconsiderate in others is seen as cheeky chappie in Our Lester. It is a strange phenomenon and it helps explain why criticising Lester Piggott has long been a certain passport to reproach.' The validity of Ashforth's case could not be disputed, even if its free expression only served to underline how waning talent and open crit-icism frequently walk hand in hand.

Any worries that Piggott might be unable to cut the mustard where it really mattered – on the back of a thoroughbred racehorse (or in his case perched a foot above it like a question mark waiting to uncoil) – were promptly dispelled by his Breeders' Cup victory on Royal Academy. The Galloping Grandfather was still good enough if the horses were good enough. He retained the nerve to go for the gaps others were afraid to explore; to wait and wait until a ridiculously late opportunity to swoop presented itself. Ice, not blood, still ran through Piggott's veins when the big races were being contested. Nor had the horseman's touch deserted him; some of the legendary strength in those arms and, especially, the legs, perhaps. But there was no substitute for experience and 40 odd years of this priceless commodity enabled him to cut a good many corners, saving a yard here and stealing a length there.

'You see it everywhere, in all walks of life', Piggott complained. 'Once you're over the age of 50, they want to replace you with a youngster, for-getting that the older person has experience and the judgement which a raw youngster will take years to acquire.' Had he made any concessions to age, he was asked at Leicester, by modifying his technique, for example? 'Nah. Same as before. One leg each side', he snorted. Later, he elucidated to Tony Stafford of the *Daily Telegraph*: 'Basically, riding in races is much the same as it always has been, although these days they go a bit quicker. Of course, when you're 50 you are not the same as when you are 30. You have lost a bit. But only just a little bit. Riding, for me, is 80 per cent skill and experience and if you are physically fit there shouldn't be any prob-lems. It's only really a question of two or three minutes work at a time. It's not as though I've got to run around a football pitch for 40 minutes. The more races you ride the better for you. I think you see what is going to happen before it happens. Even at a jockey's peak, the difference between winning and losing is only marginal, a head or a neck here and there. So much is down to the horses, that's why the top boys win the most races.'

Twelve months in prison may or may not have changed Lester Piggott's outlook on life. 'I just wonder if it did anyone any good, me going to prison. Yes, I was punished and accepted it. But did it really do anyone any good? I wouldn't have thought so.' In essence, Piggott remained his own man to the very end of his career – and in that respect he did not change at all. Lester was the same annoyingly paradoxical figure he had always been: at once confusing and irritating, his deeds adored one minute and abhorred the next. A genius untainted by arrogance. Eternally modest but frequently infuriating nonetheless. Yet this grating ambivalence was all part of the attraction. We prefer our idols with a sprinkling of devilment, a dash of salt and pepper. That face of crumpled papyrus certainly cracked more often than of old to deliver those much-loved and oft-quoted laconic *bon mots*, which, one could not avoid thinking, would be totally funny uttered by anyone else. And you had to forgive Lester because he was always so consistently egalitarian. It mattered not one jot who you were – fellow jockey, patron, administrator, journalist *et al* – Lester was a law unto himself. Every man-jack had to take the rough with the smooth; getting on with Lester meant enduring much rough for a little smooth. He pulled the strings and we danced. Right to the end. The official announcement of his retirement – no secret in the racing world – was expected to coincide with the publication of his autobiography at the time of his 60th birthday in November 1995. This 'exclusive' revelation, however, was broken in *The Mail on Sunday* of September 10th.

To be candid, no one really wanted Lester Piggott to change. It would have cheapened the alchemy, diluted the magic and, from the public's perspective at least, rendered the comeback quite pointless. The Second Coming of Lester Piggott had to be precisely that: the genuine article, the original 'Electric Horseman' appearing in the flesh, for a limited season maybe but not some rhinestone cowboy going through the motions to the sound of fake applause. For sure, Lester Piggott was not struck by some Pauline conversion on the road to or from Highpoint but, despite his own reservations to the contrary, prison affected some change in him and did him some 'good'. Of course, Lester wouldn't be Lester if he were to openly admit to such a thing or make too much show of it. As the Ashanti tribesmen of Africa insist: 'Rain beats the leopard's skin but it does not wash out the spots.'

2

REJOINING THE CIRCUS

It cannot be said that Monday, October 15th, 1990 differed very much from the thousands of other days which led back to Wednesday, April 7th, 1948, when Lester had his very first mount in public on The Chase at Salisbury. Not as far as Lester Piggott was concerned at any rate. He got up at 6am having enjoyed a good night's slumber, as ever untroubled by the prospect of a day in the saddle. A light repast of toast and fruit juice – not quite so spartan as the legendary 'cough and a copy of *The Sporting Life*' – was duly taken. Then there was work to ride. Only a fleeting glimpse of the newspaper headlines gave the game away. This was no ordinary day after all. 'Leicester Piggott' boomed the *Racing Post*: 'All roads lead to Midlands course as hero returns.' Yes, after being out of the game for five years Piggott was going to subject his 54 year-old body to the rigours of raceriding one more time. 'Good old Lester', chuckled seven-times champion Pat Eddery on hearing the news, 'He must be mad!'. While rising star Frankie Dettori had exclaimed: 'Serious? Serious? I am very pleased. I never rode with him and it was always my dream to do that.'

Eddery's incredulity was mirrored throughout the racing community. Why on earth should Lester ever contemplate such a move? Hugely respected and hugely rich, he had so much to lose and so little to gain. Why lay his reputation on the line against the new Dettori-led generation of fitter and hungrier young guns? The only feasible answer came in the form of one word: addiction. There was no other word for it – unless it was boredom, that aching feeling universally experienced by old sportsmen everywhere which once drove former soccer star Wilf Mannion to lament: 'They should shoot old pros when the time comes to hang up their boots!'

Training thoroughbreds and riding them at exercise was one thing; but riding them on the racetrack, negotiating the cut and thrust of a chess game conducted at 40 mph yielded a rush of adrenalin impossible to replicate anywhere bar a racetrack. There was no substitute for the real thing. Piggott was hooked at the age of 12 and he was still hooked three weeks short of his 55th birthday. He needed another hit. 'That adrenalin', suggested Peter O'Sullevan in the *Daily Mail*, 'will lubricate Lester's limbs, and his guts and drive will do the rest. I cannot imagine that anyone else of his vintage could make a similar comeback. The news that he was coming out of retirement was the most sensational turn of events I could imagine....but he has confounded probability in the past and it is an amazing achievement to have sustained the energy and discipline as he has done over the years.'

The seeds of Piggott's return had been germinating for a year or more. Indeed, the possibility of a riding comeback, if truth be told, had existed since 1986. Having gone into retirement (in Britain at least) at Nottingham on October 29th 1985, it had been Piggott's intention to come out of retirement barely six months later in order to ride Midway Lady and Tate Gallery in the following year's Guineas: until, that is, the plan was scuppered by contractual difficulties connected with certain memorabilia that had commemorated his 'retirement'. However, in December 1989 the opportunity arose for him to ride in an invitational event at the most improbable of venues – the Monterrico racetrack in Lima, Peru. A last-minute illness had prevented Walter Swinburn from taking up his invitation; Piggott willingly stepped into the breach; spent a day and a half in transit; and finished last on two of his three mounts. Then, the following July, he participated in the Irish Turf Club bicentenary celebrations, riding in two more invitation races at Tipperary on the 13th (Don Leone; 2nd) and the Curragh on the 15th (Legal Legend; 3rd). He was getting the taste.

As autumn approached, Vincent O'Brien, the trainer of Legal Legend and Piggott's ally in so many attacks on the world's great prizes, fed the growing appetite. 'I was on the way to Keeneland for the July Sales and was talking to my son-in-law John Magnier on the plane. He said he had been sitting next to Lester at a dinner to celebrate the bicentenary of the Turf Club. John had asked Lester what he was doing at that time and Lester said he rode out in the mornings and watched the racing on SIS in the afternoon. John suggested I should have a word with Lester about the possibility of him riding again. When I got back to Ireland I asked Lester what he felt about starting to ride again but he wasn't at all sure about it. I didn't press him at that time. A few weeks later I rang him and said why didn't he come over to Dublin so that we could have a talk. I booked a room in the Berkeley Court so that we could have dinner without having

The racing community greets its favourite prodigal son *(Dan Abraham/Racing Post)*

to worry about publicity and the result was that Lester said he would give it a go.' O'Brien promised him first choice of mounts in 1991.

The carrot was far too juicy. Raceriding seemed the sensible thing to do; it was an obsession that had to be sated. On October 9th the Jockey Club's chief medical advisor Dr Michael Allen visited Piggott's Newmarket home to give him the standard check-up for Flat jockeys over the age of 45. 'I was very impressed with Lester's condition. He's extremely fit and I had no qualms at all about passing him fit to raceride after his five-year break. He's well above average fitness for someone his age and has certainly looked after himself.'

On Thursday the 11th, Piggott applied for his licence; at 5.30pm due clearance was granted. 'Lester's Back' (*Racing Post*) and 'Lester Rides Again' (*Sporting Life*) declared Friday's front pages of the sport's two trade papers scarcely able to believe what they had printed; 'Old Stoneface rides high again' gasped another headline; 'Against All Odds' cried another. Lester would be the oldest jockey in the weighing room, assuming the mantle from 50 year-old Brian Rouse. He had, nevertheless, some years to go before emulating his 19th century predecessor Frank Buckle, who rode Classic winners at the age of 60 and had his final mount at 65; why, out in West Virginia 68 year-old Willie Clark was still going strong and riding a few winners.

As the news broke, the media sought reaction from everyone and anyone prepared to speak: family, friends, patrons, rivals – new and old.

Susan Piggott: 'I am delighted. The whole family is delighted....it took me a bit by surprise. We hadn't talked about it. But in fact I thought it was a tremendous idea. It helped that the few accidents he'd had in the 80s that were troubling him had settled down in the years he didn't ride and his weight hadn't increased. Earning money wasn't a consideration!'

Tracy Piggott: 'I am absolutely thrilled – riding horses is the only thing he has ever wanted to do. He has kept himself very fit riding out my mother's horses and he showed on a couple of recent visits to Ireland for veterans' races that he still has something to contribute. There's not so much pressure and he's doing it purely for the fun; he's fitter than I am at twice my age.'

Charles St George: 'I think Lester is bored and fit. This is the obvious course to take. I was surprised as the rest about the news. Lester had said nothing to me. It will certainly make matters more interesting for everybody involved in the sport and I would not hesitate to offer him a ride on any of my horses. I'm sure he'll have offers to ride abroad this winter and that will suit him.'

Robert Sangster: 'He'll be a welcome addition. He can certainly ride for me anytime. It's interesting coming at the end of the season. Knowing Lester, he's probably having a joke!'

Peter O'Sullevan: 'I was delighted to find him feeling relieved that the future has once again opened up for him and he will be able to renew that passionate affair he had had with the winner's circle....the ineluctable truth is that Lester cannot do without his horses. But if I were a jockey I wouldn't allow his benign, grandfatherly manner to dupe me into thinking that his will to win and competitive edge had been in any way diminished by his years away from the riding game. Punters all around the country will love to see him in action again and although I don't think it's possible for him to be as good as he was, he will still be among the best riders in the world. Given that he will never to able to recapture his youth, the status of Lester's comeback will depend on willpower and determination. And here, he is a world-beater.'

Barney Curley: 'As John Wayne said: "A man's gotta do what a man's gotta do". The most important thing in life is peace of mind.'

Joe Mercer: 'He never ceases to amaze me.'

Geoff Lewis: 'It's a bloody hard game but Lester is an extraordinary person. If anyone can do it he will and I would certainly put him on one of my horses without any hesitation.'

Jimmy Lindley: 'It's great that he's so fit but he'll still be race-rusty. It's getting the old brain working that will matter. You have to think ten times quicker in a race; it's like riding a motorbike at 100 miles an hour. His biggest problem will be getting his brain to react as quickly as it used to.'

Pat Eddery: 'I think it is marvellous news. If I know Lester he will be as fit as a flea. We had all better look out. I know he's been off for quite a while but it won't take him long to get back into the swing. I wish him all the luck in the world.'

Steve Cauthen: 'Everyone will welcome him back with open arms. Like Ali, he was the greatest.'

Bill Shoemaker: 'I won't believe it until I see it!'

Few chose such a euphoric occasion to voice reservations. Willie Carson was in a minority: 'We all wish Lester the best of luck, but I'm worried for him. It will be very hard for him after five years out of the game.' 'He went out as the greatest and I hope whatever he does now does not detract from that. In a way it is quite surprising and sad', said Walter Swinburn. Forty-seven year-old Bruce Raymond struck a similarly pragmatic note: 'He could be risking his reputation but everyone wants to see him be happy and if he's happy to ride horses again and prepared to sacrifice his past reputation just to be happy riding again then everyone will welcome him back. I don't think it'll be too difficult for him to get race-fit because he's riding every morning. The biggest thing will be the travelling and getting himself organised mentally; it'll take a few months to get sharpened up. Physically, it'll be no problem; the lay-off might just have freshened his body up. Look out for your next ride! Everybody will be very excited to give him a ride and they'll want to give him a winning ride. They'll not ask him to ride rubbish.'

Guessing the where and when of Piggott's comeback ride soon took precedence over any lingering doubts concerning its wisdom. The offer to partner Act of Diplomacy for brother-in-law Robert Armstrong in the Cartier Million at Phoenix Park on Saturday, the 13th, was politely declined. But the pieces were falling into place. Late Friday evening the phone rang. It was Charles St George. He had two unraced fillies (Lupescu and Patricia), trained by Henry Cecil, running at Leicester on the following Monday and stable jockey Steve Cauthen was feeling under the weather.

'I was discussing it with Henry, and Lester just fell into place when we realised that Steve felt he needed the day off because he was a bit flu-ey', said St George. 'Lester seems to be in good shape and he has been saying to me that the sooner people see that he's back, the better. He wants to ride that first winner and then hopefully there will be no more hassle, no more cameras and things will return to normal.'

Quite like old times: Piggott had won plenty of big races – notably on Ardross – for Cecil and St George, the two men who each put up £125,000 bail for him at the time of his trial. 'When you think about it, you could hardly start in a better way', Piggott said. 'Riding for two old friends who have done so much for you over the years. Charles said it was great news that I was riding again and that I could ride one for him at Leicester. I thought he was joking! I don't know much about the fillies and he didn't say whether or not they were expected to win but Henry doesn't put them on the track unless they've got a chance. It will be nice to get the pressure off by having these rides.' That pressure included, naturally, a press stake-out at Piggott's Newmarket bungalow which he lifted at one point by leading the press pack a merry dance round the town in his black Toyota Celica, executing U-turns worthy of Schumacher and treating a roundabout as if it were a carousel. 'I just want to ride a few races and see how I feel and go from there. I'll play it by ear. I am open to ride anywhere as long as the horses have a chance.'

The Leicester executive was prepared for a bumper crowd. 'It's terrific that he is making his comeback at Leicester', said Secretary David Henson. 'I hope he has a big effect on the crowd. Normally we get around 1,000 here on an October Monday but we're having extra racecards printed and are hoping for around 2,000'. Clerk of the Course, Nick Lees, added: 'We'll have the champagne on ice in case he rides a winner!'

The bookmaking industry steadied itself for a flood of bets on each of Piggott's three rides; he had also been engaged for Balasani by John Jenkins: 'I don't think Lester would be riding if he was not up to the task

– he is too proud to make a fool of himself. This is a big day for everybody because he is so special.' William Hill's Graham Sharpe definitely sounded a worried man: 'So many people will be backing him that even one winner would be bad for us, two would be awful and a treble an absolute disaster!' All those William Hill punters would be following the fortunes of their returning hero in the betting shops. SIS had originally planned to transmit racing from Ayr and Fontwell but after some frantic negotiations pictures from Leicester were to replace those from Fontwell. 'It's tremendous for the guy in the betting shop', said SIS racing controller George Irvine. 'He never saw Lester's retirement because TV screens weren't allowed in betting shops then but now he can see Lester's comeback.' As Ayr's race times clashed with Leicester's the Scottish course was even persuaded to delay each one until the concurrently timed race at Leicester was completed so that the cameras would miss nothing of the legend's comeback.

For many long-time Piggott devotees, an SIS screen or Racecall commentary was simply not enough: only a pilgrimage to Leicester would suffice. In such circumstances it was appropriate their number included a clergyman, David Johnson from Lutterworth: 'People say he is a scoundrel but I admire him for his professionalism. I can't ride a horse and I am sure Lester could not preach a sermon, but I admire him for the way he goes about his job.' Cheek by jowl with men of the cloth were sons of the soil, such as farmer Stanley Brothwell from Quorn: 'You are only as old as you feel and I'm delighted Lester has come back.' Then there was the market trader, Simon Reid: 'I just want Lester to go out there and prove he can do it. He's the "main man". He's come back to prove his point.' And the newsagent, Maurice Booth: 'I've been a supporter of Lester's for 40 years. I was at Nottingham when he retired and I wouldn't have missed today's comeback for all the world.'

A comfortable one-and-a-half hour drive from Newmarket, chauffeured and entertained by his wife's lightweight stable jockey Bryn Crossley, brought Piggott to Leicester's unprepossessing track, hidden amid the suburban delights of Oadby, at around 1.15pm. When they first raced here back in the 1880s, Fred Archer rode 33 winners from 75 rides before blowing his brains out in a typhoid-induced delirium a month after the last of them. On March 31st, 1921, the track saw 16 year-old Gordon Richards win his first race and it was at Oadby on November 10th, 1947, that he secured his 260th victory of the season to pass his record total of 1933. Piggott's total at Oadby stood at 172 and included a five-timer on July 19th, 1966 – one of only six he ever scored in his 38 years of riding British tracks. 'Welcome Back, Lester', it said in the race-card. Whether or not Lester won race number 173, Monday, October 15th, 1990, was surely another day bound for the Oadby archives.

However, Piggott resembled anything but the star attraction as he walked through the jockeys' entrance that afternoon. Clad in tweed jacket and grey trousers with a mackintosh over his arm, he carried a white plastic bag that contained his boots and breeches; only the dark glasses on an overcast afternoon hinted at celebrity. The magnetic effect his appearance exerted on the assorted camera crews and autograph hunters who barred his path to the weighing room instantly raised the temperature. Enduring such ordeals had never exactly been Piggott's cup of tea. He smiled a lot, muttered a little and basically suffered in silence until reaching the haven that is the weighing room. There he could resume normal service within an environment and a brotherhood he both knew and trusted. His old valet, Brian York, promptly divested him of the plastic carrier bag while several of the senior jockeys – including the demoted 'old man' Brian Rouse – bade him welcome. 'I feel young today. Lester's taken years off me', joked Rouse. 'There's still a deep affection for Lester. We're all really pleased to see him back – it seems more like five weeks than five years', added John Williams.

Fortunately, neither Piggott nor the crowd, fast approaching 3,000, has long to wait for the historic comeback ride: Lupescu's race, the Hare Maiden Fillies Stakes (Division One) over seven furlongs, is the first race on the card at 2.15pm. Piggott carries his 3lb saddle through to the scales to weigh out; behind him the press photographers look like a bunch of monkeys as they scrabble to get their cameras against the plate-glass window of the weighing room and snap the shot all their picture editors would be demanding.

For a second time, Lester runs the gauntlet of media spotlight and public adulation – on this occasion fortified by a police escort – en route to the paddock; the ritualistic folding of arms and faraway look precedes a leg up on to Lupescu from Henry Cecil's representative Simon Bray. Piggott was back where he belonged. If any cares remain, they are despatched during the splendid isolation of cantering to post.

Down at the start Lester finds many of the same handlers who attended his last ride at Nottingham. It is Roy Gamlin who has the honour of leading Lupescu into stall seven; she needs a helping shove. 'Lester looked just the same and said just as little. He never has been much of a conversationalist.' Piggott's gimlet eyes survey the nine rivals to his left and right. The favourite, at odds on, is Sumonda, from the stable of close pal Geoff

The gates spring open and the years roll back: Lupescu breaks quicker than Carousella (Brett Doyle) to her left *(Trevor Jones)*

The cries of 'Come on, Lester!' are not enough to conjure up the fairytale ending: Lupescu fails by a short head *(Dan Abraham/Racing Post)*

Back in the fold at a lunch for winners of the Ritz Club Trophy: (left to right)
Walter Swinburn, Steve Cauthen, Lester, Joe Mercer, Willie Carson and Pat Eddery
(Edward Whitaker/Racing Post)

Wragg, and ridden by young Gary Carter, still a 5lb claimer when Piggott last rode.

Up in the stands binoculars are focussed. Among the mesmerised are Maureen and Tracy Piggott. Maureen's husband, William Haggas, has a runner in the race; although divided loyalties are impossible in a situation like this. Susan Piggott is absent: she is otherwise engaged at the Newmarket October Sales. 'Trust Lester!' she says. 'He chose to have his last ride before he packed up right in the middle of the horses-in-training sale where I was busy. Then he picks the October yearling sale for his comeback. How typical!' Lester's back in the groove, all right.

They're off! The Michael Roberts-ridden Yasmeen Valley leads from the gate tracked by Lupescu and the favourite. The 'Piggott Perch' – the angle and height of the posterior – conveys to experienced Piggott watchers the fact that Lupescu is travelling smoothly. With two furlongs to run, Lester's posterior drops into the saddle and he draws his whip. Which implement would it be today? Will it be the persuader or the magic wand? We watch transfixed. On a debutante filly there would be no repeat of the famous 11-stroke rat-a-tat-tat machine-gunned on to Roberto's rump in order to win the 1972 Derby. Tenderly applying the bare minimum of force Lester coaxes Lupescu past Yasmeen Valley. Instinctively the old war cry of 'Come on Lester!' rolls down the course from the enclosures to greet him – until the sight of Sumonda closing fast on the stands side unites the

20

yells into a single roar that can be heard two miles away at Leicester's Clock Tower. Lupescu shows her greenness by edging left towards the challenger who, benefiting from two runs (one of them a decent fourth place in the Group I Cheveley Park only twelve days earlier), knows a tad more about the game through the final furlong. The pair flash past the post locked together; 'Photograph! Photograph!' booms the tannoy, soon adding 'Stewards' Enquiry' for good measure. 'He's a freak', declares Barney Curley. 'How can a man miss five years and ride a finish like that?'

The photo, as most realised, went against Lupescu by a short head. The enquiry likewise went as most knew it would if Lester Piggott was involved. Beforehand the senior steward at the meeting, Lord Gainsborough, shook the jockey's hand and welcomed him back. Lester, his face wreathed in smiles, said 'Thank you', went into the stewards' room, mumbled 'The filly ran a bit green' and walked out again. As deadpan as ever in the face of authority; definitely no change there.

Nor was his subsequent treatment of the baying hacks clamouring for an audience. Sheltering beneath the only available umbrella, Lester delivered one-liners and platitudes as if he'd never been away, doubtless amused by the willingness of his inquisitors to get soaked for the privilege. Had he altered his riding technique? 'Nah. Same as before. One leg either side.' How could he conceivably make such a low weight after the lay-off? 'Missed Sunday lunch.' Did you think you'd win? 'I thought for a second I was going to. Gary came to beat me and then I nearly got back at him but she got tired in the last few strides and the experience told. It was great to get so close. I was frightened I might be last. I'm pretty fit. I was a bit surprised at how fit I was. I was amazed at how easy it was out there, though I'm bound to need a race or two under my belt to get race-fit. My weight has been very good for most of the summer. If it hadn't been I wouldn't have thought of making a comeback. I was able to use a 3lb saddle and still did 8st 11lb.'

Balasani (a cranky character; finished 7th) in the fourth race and Patricia (disappointing; beat only four) in the last were unable to give the fairytale its prescribed happy ending. In actual fact, the afternoon belonged not to Piggott but to Walter Swinburn, who completed a five-timer. 'I almost wish Lester had won one of them. Never mind, he won't have long to wait.' At least Lester's presence gained Swinburn some consolation: the champagne reserved for a Piggott winner was given to him instead.

While this was going on Piggott nipped out of the weighing room's back door in an effort to avoid further hounding by the media. He had illuminated an increasingly murky afternoon and had already provided soundbites a-plenty. Every television news bulletin transmitted the pictures that evening.

Tuesday's papers were, needless to say, chock-a-block with Piggott, front page and back, broadsheet and tabloid. 'It's just like the old days as Lester gives a vintage show' (*Daily Telegraph*); 'Return of the King' (*Daily Mail*). As for the trades, the *Racing Post* responded with 'Back with all the old magic/Just great to have you back, Lester/Piggott mania in the betting shops' spread over four pages.

Until Steve Cauthen's bout of flu Piggott had intended to make his comeback on October 16th at Chepstow, partnering Nicholas for his wife in the Biddestone All-Aged Stakes over six furlongs. So many years had slid by since Piggott last rode at Chepstow that crossing the Severn Bridge amounted to something of a novelty. Arriving at the course, he dodged a second crush by slipping inside as the first race was being run and, after coming last on Ruddy Cheek in the three o'clock, he just as easily slipped into the old winning routine aboard Nicholas. Switching his mount two off the rail at the furlong marker to launch his challenge outside Amigo Menor and Restore, the 6–4 favourite scored a mite cheekily by half a length. 'I decided to give him a good chance to settle and tracked the first three. He had ten stone to carry and the ground was a little soft. He ran a little lazily when he hit the front so I had to ride him but I was always confident.'

Among the throng who watched Piggott being presented with a Chepstow goblet and a bottle of champagne was the senior steward of the Jockey Club, Lord Hartington. 'Among the leading jockeys there are some wonderful people with whom the racegoing public can identify. Lester ranks with the highest of these. He has always been a star.'

More – significantly more – was to follow in the next race. Eric Eldin's Shining Jewel, noted as a difficult horse to place and winless after ten attempts, hardly knew he had had a race as Piggott quietly brought him through to win the second division of the Gainsborough Claiming Stakes by two-and-a-half lengths without seeming to have activated a single muscle. This really did revive memories of yesteryear's 'Peerless Piggott' tag and justify its resurrection on the *Racing Post*'s front page.

Lester was back, make no mistake. This was no one-off. The comeback was in deadly earnest. There was further evidence of a totally irrefutable nature. Lester had gone out and spent money on a new pair of riding boots. He must mean business.

3

THE OLD FIRM

It is hugely fitting that Vincent O'Brien, the greatest of all Irish trainers and one of Ireland's finest ambassadors, should have been so instrumental in luring Lester Piggott back into the saddle on a full-time basis. The Irish loved Lester Piggott. This undying romance was, to be sure, perfectly understandable. In the 'land of the horse' was it not perfectly natural to worship the closest thing to a centaur the modern world could offer? The depth of Piggott idolatry in Ireland is nicely encapsulated in a story related by Irish jockey Richard Fox. One day at the Curragh a fellow wandered into a weighing room clutching five or six racing prints, which he asked Piggott to sign. 'It'll cost you, you know'. Having got a positive reply Piggott signed and went out to ride. 'You didn't pay the old so-and-so, did you?', enquired Pat Eddery, who was standing nearby. 'Sure it doesn't matter', said the contented interloper, 'I'll get five grand for them at Galway next week!'

Perhaps it says something about the character of the Irish people, their forgiving spirit or their easy-going nature, above all, their infatuation with the Turf and its denizens, but Piggott was welcomed back into the fold like some long-lost son who had made it big on the far side of the Atlantic. Wherever he went in the Emerald Isle people turned up in droves. He became the Pied Piper of Irish racing. From Down Royal in the north east to Tralee and Killarney in the south west, the Piggott roadshow smashed attendance records. 'He gets a tremendous kick out of riding these places', said Tracy Piggott. 'It has given him a real taste of the special atmosphere of Irish racing and, of course, there's nothing that compares with the way people show their feelings in Ireland. You've just got to see the beaming faces to realise what it means to them.'

Piggott's return to Down Royal on November 3rd, 1990, after a 23-year absence – his only previous visit was to win the 1967 Ulster Derby on Dan Kano – boosted the attendance to something near 3,000 according

Lester takes the reins for a jaunt around Killarney's lakes accompanied by Barney
Curley and Finbarr Slattery *(Don Macmonagle/Racing Post)*

to course manager Ian Duff. 'We got roughly two-and-a-half times our usual crowd for this time of year. Bringing Lester here was certainly worthwhile. It created quite a buzz and brought many people who have never before gone racing.' Piggott was applauded every time he ventured out of the weighing room and the reception he got in the unsaddling enclosure after finishing a remote second on each of his two mounts bettered those accorded the actual winners.

The following summer saw Piggott pay his first ever visit to Killarney, taking five rides on the evening meeting of July 15, the opening day of the four-day festival – thereby fulfilling the lifelong ambition of manager Finbarr Slattery to get Piggott to ride at the picturesque Kerry track. The Piggott magic delivered. A record first-day crowd approaching 6,000 witnessed 'Yer Man' land a well-backed treble on Defendant (4–5 favourite), News Headlines (5–4 favourite) and Classic Trust (11–8 favourite), all trained by Vincent O'Brien.

A week later, on July 22, and it was the turn of little Ballinrobe in the west of Ireland to have its moment in the sun. The tiny County Mayo venue was another track being explored for the first time by Piggott. The job of snaring the biggest catch around fell to Peter Costello, chairman of the Ballinrobe Supporters' Club. 'Ballinrobe is a remote spot and so anything going does not normally come as far as us. We have to go out and get it. My brief is to get people through the turnstiles and Piggott is still the biggest attraction in racing. We've made arrangements for him to fly into Knock airport and stay the night at Ashford Castle Hotel. We plan to fix him up with rides in the three Flat races that evening and there will be an appearance fee as well.' Despite poor weather 4,500 crammed into Ballinrobe, an increase of 2,000 on the previous best. Piggott did not disappoint the fans. A typically forceful display on his second ride of the night saw the 11–8 favourite Miss Mittens forge clear to win by five lengths.

Four festivals dominate summer racing in western Ireland: Killarney, Galway, Listowel and Tralee. On August 23rd, 1993, Piggott dropped in on the last named. The effect was entirely predictable. 'Lester, the toast of Tralee', reported *The Sporting Life*; 'Piggott pulls them in by the thousand', declared the *Daily Mail*.

The six-day Festival at Ballybeggan Park is held to coincide with The Rose of Tralee beauty pageant when girls of Irish descent jet in from all over the world to compete against Kerry girls in the televised contest, the winner being paraded along the finishing straight of the racecourse. The atmosphere is akin to one, week-long Mardi Gras, or as the Irish would describe it, a hooley to end all hooleys. The hooley commenced at the traditional Roses Parade around the town three days before the racing even got underway and featured a Piggott lookalike being driven about in a soft-top Volkswagen. One lady rang the local radio station to clarify if it was or wasn't the great man himself! On the Monday evening it seemed as if the whole of County Kerry had converged on Ballybeggan Park to confirm the identity of the man in the emerald green and red silks walking out to ride the Aga Khan's Caliandak in the O'Cathain IASC Maiden Stakes. Fathers nodded sagely toward young sons before lifting them head high so that fresh faces might gaze upon a legend in the flesh. Piggott's name beside Caliandak's number caused the 3YO's odds to shrink from 11–8 against to 5–4 on and every one of the favourite's supporters must have believed the game was up when the gelding appeared to be labouring entering the final half mile. Then the old stands began to shake as Piggott got to work. Spotting a gap between Alyrey and Uncertain Affair – partnered by the two top riders in Ireland, Christy Roche and Michael Kinane – Piggott gave Caliandak one crack with the 'Piggott Persuader' and it was all over. The favourite shot through to win by half a length.

Pat Green left the course, another in a lengthening line of happy Irish track secretaries. 'Lester has helped launch the Festival magnificently with at least 2,000 more on the gate, an increase of nearly 25 per cent, on what is normally a quiet day. If he comes to the Curragh it wouldn't add 200 to the crowd in all probability but Lester coming to Tralee has given the meeting a real boost and there is a real buzz around the town. Tote turnover was up by IR£28,000 on last year's takings and in the Ring IR£345,000 was wagered compared to IR£266,000 a year ago.'

The shot in the arm to Irish racing provided by Piggott's comeback demanded recognition. It was not long coming. The Racing Club of Ireland made him the 1991 recipient of the Par Excellence Award for outstanding contributions to the sport, following in the footsteps of such notables as Vincent O'Brien, Pat Taaffe and Michael O'Hehir. 'It is fitting that he should win the award because it is designed to reward outstanding contributions to racegoers' enjoyment over the years', said chairman Kevin Smith. 'Lester has given tremendous excitement to racing fans in Ireland in a long career and his popularity can be witnessed every time he rides here.' Making the presentation at the awards dinner in September at the Red House Inn, Newbridge, Smith added: 'I hope Rudyard Kipling will smile gently on the very small alteration I need to make to his work – for you have met with triumph and disaster and treated those two imposters just the same. You have indeed filled an unforgiving minute with 60-seconds worth of distance run. And, which is more, you are the man, Lester, my son!'

Piggott's response was typically short but typically 'dry' rather than sweet. Most of it was lost amid riotous laughter. 'It's just as well you Irish look after your horses', he chided, 'because the only thing you have more of is potatoes!'

Notwithstanding the award's citation for a lifetime's contribution to the enjoyment of Irish racegoers, Piggott's riding record in this initial year of the comeback merited an accolade in its own right. In the 12 months following his return to competitive Irish racing at the Curragh on October 23rd, 1990, Piggott rode 27 winners from 91 mounts, 24 of them provided (from 56 opportunities) by O'Brien. Indeed, O'Brien's Portico, at the Curragh on October 12th, 1991, was Piggott's 200th Irish winner – some 33 years after the first, Rise Above at Phoenix Park on April 9th, 1958.

The highly emotional autumn of 1990 was particularly fruitful for the resurrected 'Old Firm' of Piggott and O'Brien, rekindling fond memories of the halcyon period when they seemingly plundered Europe's greatest prizes at will. Their opening gambit all those years ago was a winner in an event of Group I calibre: Gladness in the 1958 Ascot Gold Cup. However, the association really fired in the 1960s and 70s after Piggott had turned freelance: nine English Classics; six Irish Classics; two Prix de l'Arc de Triomphes; 15 Royal Ascot winners; four July Cups; five Dewhursts; three Sussex Stakes; two Eclipses; two King Georges; two Champion Stakes; a Coronation Cup; a Middle Park; a Cheveley Park; a Grand Criterium; an Observer Gold Cup. Plus a Washington International in the United States: all Group I events. A staggering haul reflecting a fearsome combination of talent. Consequently, when stable jockey John Reid was injured on the afternoon of the 1990 Arc there were no prizes for guessing who would be invited to replace him on Ballydoyle's choicest representatives.

Accordingly, on Tuesday October 23rd – just eight days after the comeback kicked off at Leicester – 54-year old Piggott and 73-year old O'Brien teamed up at the Curragh. 'It was like having a Derby runner; I was so apprehensive', the legendary trainer told the press. He might have consoled himself with the reassuring thought that his 'runners' had, after all, won six Derbies – four aided by Lester Keith Piggott.

The afternoon scotched any notion that the Galloping Grandfather might have lost a bit of his guile and too much of his strength to survive in a younger man's world. The crowd were in for a box of delights. O'Brien legged Piggott up on to four runners. All four won. Quite unbe-

Four whacks in the last four strides and Royal Academy prevails by a neck *(Trevor Jones)*

lievable: quite memorable. It was vintage Piggott. Legal Profession (by a cosy four lengths); Fairy Folk (lifted home by a head); Classic Minstrel (holding on by three-quarters of a length after stealing a march on the turn); and Passer-By (a late pounce to win going away by two-and-a-half lengths).

At Leopardstown's Bank Holiday meeting six days later, the *Racing Post* was pleased to report that 'The Piggott and O'Brien show rolls on' as Judicial Wit won the Bailey's Mile Maiden; and then, on November 7th at the Curragh, Law Chambers gave the rejuvenated combo its sixth Irish success in nine attempts. However glittering, this Irish blitz failed to tell the whole story for a seventh victory, and the most miraculous victory of all, had come courtesy of Royal Academy in the Breeders' Cup Mile at Belmont Park, New York, on Saturday October 27th.

The enormity of Piggott's achievement on that sharp, sunlit New York afternoon cannot be overstressed. To win any race at the Breeders' Cup is an extraordinary feat. Even in his pomp Piggott would have excelled himself to have notched a victory on this phenomenally competitive day's racing. Of the 42 races held during the six-year series, European competitors had won just five; more significantly, the British contribution to this paltry total was one and Ireland's nil. Nor had any English jockey got on the scoresheet. Piggott's appearances, naturally, had been limited by his five-year absence coinciding with the development of the meeting as a major autumn showpiece. His single mount, Theatrical, finished 11th in the 1985 Turf – ironically behind Britain's sole winner, the filly Pebbles.

Royal Academy flew out of Shannon Airport on a chartered jet three days before the race accompanied by O'Brien's travelling head lad, Gerry Gallagher; the trainer himself was confined to Ballydoyle by a bout of flu, leaving his wife Jacqueline and son Charles to represent him. 'Royal Academy seems to be very fresh, which must be a big advantage at this late stage of the season,' 'Charles informed the American press. 'After all, he's had only four races this year.'

A $3.5 million son of the great O'Brien-Piggott champion Nijinsky, the Triple Crown winner of 1970, Royal Academy had had a mixed season: Group III Tetrarch Stakes over seven furlongs (won; three lengths); Group I Irish 2,000 Guineas over a mile (second; beaten a neck); Group I St James's Palace Stakes over a mile (refused to enter stalls); Group I July Cup over six furlongs (won; three-quarters of a length); Group I Ladbroke Sprint Cup over six furlongs (second; beaten one-and-a-half lengths). 'Royal Academy needs switching off and riding from behind and we have got the right man for the job. He'll keep Royal Academy switched off at the back. He needs a confident jockey like Lester and wouldn't have been suited by an American jockey.'

Royal Academy was owned by Classic Thoroughbreds, a public company set up by O'Brien and Sangster to compete with the Arabs in the sales rings of the world. However, the company was feeling the pinch. It needed a big winner – badly. Not every shareholder was keen to see the company's immediate financial prospects in the hands of a jockey with only 23 rides to his name in the last five years. Piggott understood: 'Vincent needed a lot of faith to give me the ride. Hell of a lot. There were four others who might have had the ride before me.'

Charles O'Brien's co-operative and articulate replies to their enquiries may have impressed the members of the American media but, true to form, Piggott's did not. Lester duly gave them a regal wave from the rear of his black Cadillac as it purred through the entrance to Belmont's 'back-stretch' training complex but that is as much as anyone got. The British journalists in attendance were used to existing on a starvation diet of quotes from Old Stoneface but this nonchalant attitude toward media exposure baffled their American counterparts who were more familiar with sportsmen all too eager for self-promotion. Piggott had never forgotten or ever forgiven the American press for the slating it gave him for his riding of Sir Ivor in the 1968 Washington International and Dahlia in the same race six years later: 'Limey bum' was one of the more printable phrases. Donning a pale blue anorak and bright red cap, Piggott eased Royal Academy through one circuit of the dirt track and kept his counsel. Lester may have nonplussed the Americans but he was not fooling anyone else. 'Lester left nothing undone to make victory as certain as possible', said Jacqueline O'Brien. 'He walked the track carefully and spent every possible moment with the horse.' Some local hacks took instant revenge, it seemed, by mangling the story (he had been released from prison only the previous week, according to the *New York Times*) and misspelling his name (Piggot); even so, six of the top 22 tipsters believed Piggott and Royal Academy could prevail and lift the $450,000 first prize. 'Royal Academy's the Longshot Special', proposed Mike Marten in *Daily Racing Form*, the bible of the American Turf.

Marten's hunch proved wonderfully accurate, though Royal Academy actually wound up the 5–2 favourite rather than a 'longshot' on an afternoon which all who were in attendance – and indeed an awful lot more who watched on television – declared was the greatest day's racing they had ever witnessed. It was an afternoon which pulled the heartstrings this way and that: from agony to ecstasy by way of horror in a matter of minutes; 'Racing's Darkest Day', pronounced the *New York Times*.

Three horses died. In the Sprint, Mr Nickerson collapsed from a suspected heart attack in the backstretch, bringing down Shaker Knit with fatal consequences. Even worse was to follow in the Distaff, the most eagerly anticipated event of the day which pitted the west coast's 6YO Bayakoa, the reigning Distaff queen, against the east's darling, the 3YO Go for Wand, the previous year's heroine of the Juvenile Fillies and the winner of her last five races, all Grade Is. After running neck and neck for the best part of a mile, the duo were pounding down the stretch when Go for Wand suddenly stumbled and cartwheeled through the inside rail; her right foreleg had snapped. In full view of the stands bursting with 51,236 people – most of whom had been rooting for her – the terror-stricken filly scrambled to her feet and careered on toward the finish wire in pursuit of the other runners, her irreparably damaged foreleg swinging grotesquely. Quickly brought down by an outrider, New York's favourite racehorse was immediately put to sleep; Go for Wand's life ebbed away with her head lying across the wire.

As Royal Academy and the rest went to post 30 minutes later the track was still in a state of total shock. Racegoers were openly weeping. The overwhelming sense of grief was suffocating and had to be experienced to be believed. The meeting desperately required a lift. The British contingent in the crowd were no less affected. In addition, it had seen its champion sprinter Dayjur lose the ill-fated Sprint as a direct result of jumping two shadows that fell across the bright orange dirt just prior to the finish line. Nothing could really expunge the mind-numbing images of the previous hour but Lester Piggott and Royal Academy did their best.

The principal obstacle in their path was the defending champion Steinlen, while Priolo and Markofdistinction were other Europeans holding Group I-winning credentials. All American races invariably exhibit very fast pace out of the starting gate; speed beyond the dreams of European runners. Given Royal Academy's slow-starting predilections to boot, it was obvious Lester would be obliged to sit and suffer early on in the hope of picking up the leaders close home. If the Americans went too fast for their own good all the better, because the leaders would palpably be tiring.

As expected, Royal Academy broke last of the 13 runners and Expensive Decision, who had set a new world record for the mile on grass at Belmont the previous month, went straight into the lead with the apparent aim of lowering it. But he was travelling a shade too fast: the factions of 22.6 for the quarter and 45.8 for the half which flashed on to the trackside teletimer said as much. He would never maintain that tempo for the whole mile. At the top of the stretch, Expensive Decision began to falter. Itsallgreektome got to him. The Brits and the Irish in the stands were paying scant attention to this tussle, however. Their eyes were glued to Royal Academy shooting past horse after horse on the wide outside. Lester's long right arm, growing longer with each blow, rose and fell ten times. With 100 yards to run, victory looked a possibility: 50 yards from the wire it became an inevitability. Four whacks in the last four strides; the verdict was a neck. 'The living legend out of retirement! 54 year-old Lester Piggott pulls off the upset here!' bawled course commentator Tom Durkin.

In what seemed a trice Piggott was beating a path through the tribe of ecstatic supporters to undergo the ritual of a post-race interview for Channel 4 at the microphone of Brough Scott. The Stoneface cracked into a beaming grin revealing Belmont mud still sticking to his teeth. 'Even by his standards this has just about capped it all', Scott had been enthusing. 'I hate the word genius, but with Lester you can't avoid it.'

Lester, not for the first time, had saved the day: 'I knew I needed a lot of luck and I had it. And I had a good horse. He was a bit slow out of the gate because he had a man holding him on the inside. It wasn't a bad thing

The living legend tells Brough Scott and all the Channel 4 viewers back home how it was done (Trevor Jones)

being behind early because they went too fast and after halfway I was able to pick them up and get into a good position. Then, just before we straightened up he ducked a bit – he put his foot in a hole or ducked at a shadow or something – and lost all his momentum. It took him another 50 yards to get going again. He'd have won a bit further otherwise.'

Like everyone else who saw it, the connections of Royal Academy were overawed by Lester's bravura display. A breathless Charles O'Brien, who had been waving his arms as demonically as Piggott toward the finish, said: 'When you write the story no one will believe it; it's so amazing. We've had this race in mind for Royal Academy all year. The mile on turf tracks over here always gears itself toward a sprint horse rather than the genuine miler or a one-and-a-quarter mile horse coming back to a mile. He was only beaten a neck in the Irish Guineas in May and we felt with improvement through the year he had a good chance of staying the mile today.'

O'Brien's mother then voiced the thoughts of many: 'The greatest thrill for Vincent is having Lester ride the horse.' The feeling was mutual. Piggott knew the risk O'Brien had taken in putting him up. Had the gamble come unstuck the trainer would have felt the heat. 'It was a fairy tale. It was an unbelievable day, really. It meant so much to everyone. Those sort of days are marvellous days.'

The Americans love a winner, so it was no surprise to see Lester feted in Sunday's newspapers. Never let it be said the press lets a grudge get in the way of a good story. The *New York Newsday* referred to 'A "Royal" Comeback for Piggott'; *Metro Turf* called it 'One of the great racing comebacks of all time'. In the *Daily Racing Form*, Marten likened it to 'a comeback that could only be topped if Bill Shoemaker were to come out of retirement and win the Kentucky Derby again.'

Back in Britain, the tragedy of three dead racehorses was understandably played down. 'Bedlam prevails as vintage Piggott lifts Academy home', reported the *Racing Post*. Inside, Paul Haigh expanded: 'Something had to take away the taste of horror...Lester Piggott and Vincent O'Brien just about did it. Figures from history came back to make history again.' Numerous tributes in similar vein flooded in from every section of the racing community.

Jonjo O'Neill: 'I beat him in a veterans' race at Tipperary and he's riding so well that I'm thinking about making a comeback myself! It's fantastic because that fella has a glimmer back in his eye...he is like a kid with a new toy.'

Brian Rouse: 'It was magic. It just shows what you can do when you've got the confidence. Those four winners at the Curragh would have put him on cloud nine.'

Robert Armstrong: 'It was absolutely marvellous, a vintage Piggott ride, the sort you have expected to see over the last 40 years.'

Barney Curley: 'It was like something out of fantasy land, wasn't it? I don't think anyone else would have won on the horse.'

Peter O'Sullevan: 'With just one ride Lester revived all the memories of those great finishes and this one needed Lester at his very best.'

The Old Firm enjoyed three more seasons before O'Brien, at the age of 77, retired at the end of 1994. Each of those three seasons was marked by success in Irish Pattern races. In 1991 they won five, most notably El Prado's Group I National Stakes, the country's premier event for 2YO colts. The big, grey son of former O'Brien Irish Guineas winners Sadler's Wells and Lady Capulet tended to carry his head high and was no easy ride ('He's not as dedicated as you or I', Piggott informed O'Brien after the

National) yet Piggott also got him to win the Railway (Group III) and the Beresford Stakes (Group II). 'Considering his size he's done very well so far', Piggott conceded. 'If he gets his act together he could be anything.' Alas, El Prado sprained a joint the following spring and never ran again.

After winning his first two races of 1991 it appeared that Sportsworld might conceivably represent the Piggott-O'Brien combination in the Derby, and Irish money backed him from 66–1 down to 20s. However, the trainer considered the colt too inexperienced (he was unraced as a juvenile) and kept him back for the Irish Derby. Sportsworld made all to win his trial – the Group II Gallinule – and started third favourite for the Classic but proved out of his depth behind the English and French Derby winners Generous and Suave Dancer. The remaining success of 1991 came via Archway in the Group III Greenlands Stakes.

Piggott's allegiance to the Master of Ballydoyle did backfire on one occasion. Having partnered the Irish filly Kooyonga, trained by O'Brien's former assistant Michael Kauntze, to finish second in the 1,000 Guineas at Newmarket, he abandoned her for the Irish equivalent in favour of O'Brien's unbeaten Rua D'Oro, on whom he had won the Guineas trial at Leopardstown. Made a 2–1 favourite to win Piggott his 16th Irish Classic, Rua D'Oro moved up menacingly in the straight only to drop away tamely as Kooyonga surged to a spectacular victory. Whether Piggott's loyalty to O'Brien would have survived the rumoured opportunity to ride Suave Dancer in the Irish Derby had Cash Asmussen not recovered in time from a broken collar bone is another matter altogether.

Seldom a year passed without O'Brien unveiling at least one highly promising 2YO and 1992 was to prove no exception. The animal in question was Fatherland, another beautifully bred colt by Sadler's Wells out of yet another former star O'Brien female, the 1974 Coronation Stakes winner Lisadell. Running in the colours of Jacqueline O'Brien, Fatherland won his first four races, including the Futurity and the National (which registered the 47th Group I success for the Piggott-O'Brien team and featured a typically whirlwind last to first inside the final 50 yards finish from the rider). Then, in the Dewhurst, Fatherland ran into a real hot-pot in the shape of Zafonic and could muster only a disappointing fifth place. Anticlimax continued in 1993. He was beaten in both his trial for the Irish 2,000 Guineas (he was found to have muck in his lungs) and the Classic itself, although he got to within a head of catching Barathea. However, Fatherland's name will crop up in many a quiz for he became the ninth and last standard bearer of the Old Firm in the Derby in the wake of Right Noble (1966: 9th); Sir Ivor (1968: won); Nijinsky (1970:

won); Roberto (1972: won); Cavo Doro (1973: 2nd); The Minstrel (1977: won); Inkerman (1978: 21st); and Monteverdi (1980: 14th).

When they first teamed up, Piggott frequently received copious written instructions from O'Brien and there was a degree of electricity between them. Both used spoken words sparingly. Communications improved with a burgeoning mutual respect. 'I always talked with Lester before a Derby but I didn't lay down any exact instructions. He has known all the horses he has ridden for me there and nobody knows Epsom better than Lester.' Indeed, O'Brien was responsible for two memorable testaments to Piggott's uncanny ability around Epsom. The great charm of having Lester ride for you, he said, was that it got him off the other fellow's horse; and on a more analytical occasion he suggested Lester was worth 7lb in a Derby. Fatherland would need all of that 7lb if he was to figure in the shake up of the 1993 renewal.

Although a foot abcess may not have helped the colt's preparation, he and Piggott had no excuses on the day; they were just never in the firing line. At the top of the hill Fatherland had just four horses behind him and Piggott was already beginning to niggle at him. He was not handling Epsom's undulations, according to his rider. They trailed in ninth of the 16, some 21 lengths behind Commander In Chief. After a race in France, Fatherland was sent to be trained in the USA, where he broke a pastern in the Hollywood Derby and was destroyed.

'A Genius and the Greatest': if one talks, the other listens *(Trevor Jones)*

An historic chapter was closing. In October 1992 Piggott gave O'Brien's Andros Bay an inspired ride to win the Group II Blandford Stakes at the Curragh. The 3YO's previous race had been in modest company at Listowel and en route to the start he also unshipped Piggott – and spent the next two minutes evading all attempts at recapture. Reunited with Piggott, the obstreperous beast was sent to the front a long way out, eventually began to hang fire and was fast pulling himself up as challengers bore down on him toward the line. Only a drop of the Piggott brew combining strength and cunning in equal portions got the bay colt home by half a length.

The Old Firm's last throw of the dice turned out to be with College Chapel, a strong, good-looking bay, son of the champion sprinter Sharpo, running in the red and white silks of Jacqueline O'Brien. Unraced at two years, College Chapel – one of only eleven horses at Ballydoyle in 1993 – made a sensational entry to racing by winning the Group III Tetrarch Stakes as the 12–1 outsider of six with Willie Supple in the saddle. Very few horses win Pattern races on their debuts. Piggott was aboard for the Greenlands and victory there set up a visit to Royal Ascot for the Cork & Orrery (Group III) over six furlongs. College Chapel had 18 to beat, among them an Abbaye winner in Keen Hunter: burdened as he was by an 8lb penalty for his two Group victories to date, College Chapel would need to be of Group I calibre himself in order to win. Punters were in no doubt: within an hour of the Hill's offices opening for business his price of 6–1 was cut to 9–2; another hour and it was 7–2. Piggott set out to nurse the inexperienced colt, keeping a tight hold of his head until the sixth furlong. Pouncing on Keen Hunter with 150 yards to go, College Chapel strode to a cosy one-length victory.

It was O'Brien's 25th winner at the Royal meeting (the 1956 Jersey Stakes won by Adare having been the first) the Piggott's 117th (Malka's Boy, in the 1952 Wokingham had done the honours in his case). This was their 18th in tandem; and would, moreover, constitute each man's last. 'Last Royal hurrah for the Old Firm?' asked *The Sporting Life*'s headline. With such a prospect in the offing, O'Brien was cajoled into leading-in his winner, the first occasion this most reserved of men had consented to such an extravagant gesture since Nijinsky's King George of 1970. Broad smiles abounded along with the cheers. 'Return of the warriors', was how the *Daily Mail* chose to describe the highly-charged moment. 'Lester said he was still inexperienced. That's the first time he's really had to race and it will have taught him a lot; he was floundering a little in the ground. I think that must have been a Group I performance. I thought he had a lot to do with his penalties. I could supplement him for the July Cup. When the entries opened in February he hadn't even had a run; he was weak and had some minor problems as a 2YO.'

O'Brien did supplement College Chapel for the Group I July Cup three weeks later. Sent off the 9–4 favourite, he never got in a blow at the front-running Hamas and was beaten three lengths into second. Piggott felt his draw cost him the race: 'He was badly drawn against the rail whereas the winner had the advantage of the better ground out in the middle of the course.' College Chapel bounced straight back, however, by taking the Group II Prix Maurice de Gheest at Deauville. Unfortunately, hopes that he would develop with maturity, like his sire, into a champion sprinter were dashed. He won just once more – the 1994 Greenlands – before his career ended with a sound thrashing in the Cork & Orrery.

That 1994 Greenlands proved the final Pattern race winner in the monumental career of Vincent O'Brien: on October 5th he announced his retirement. Tributes had to be glowing if they were to do justice to the departure of one of the truly great figures in the history of the Turf. They were. The *Racing Post*, for example, carried a 12-page supplement. 'I rode my first winner for Vincent nearly 40 years ago and he has been part of my life ever since', said Piggott. 'He was the man who gave me the most encouragement to return to raceriding. I would not have thought about it otherwise. In my opinion he is the greatest trainer of all time.' And O'Brien's opinion of his long-time ally? 'When you talk of Lester Piggott you must talk in superlatives. To me, he was a genius.'

There you have it. The Greatest and a Genius; a Genius and the Greatest.

Let the two people who probably monitored the Old Firm's progress closer than anybody else have the final words on the subject. Robert Sangster: 'Vincent's partnership with Lester worked so well because both men had such respect for each other. Neither of them suffered fools. They would grunt at each other and Vincent was one of the few people Lester would listen to.' Jacqueline O'Brien: 'Vincent never had much time for idle chat and none at all for gossip. On the other hand, if there was one phrase in a conversation that interested him he would switch on immediately. He could always hear what Lester said, no matter how softly or indistinctly, because he wanted to hear it.'

The tide of time was turning. Piggott's last mount in the 'land of the horse' was Tourandot, half an hour after Bin Ajwaad's Desmond Stakes victory at the Curragh on 13th August, 1995. The Irish romance initiated by Rise Above was finally at an end.

4

ROUTING THE SCEPTICS

With the sweat still frothing on Lupescu's heaving flanks as she stood in the space reserved for the runner-up in Leicester's unsaddling enclosure, an uncharitable voice was heard to sneer: 'Five years ago he would have won that easily.' Despite the virtuoso performance on Royal Academy, Piggott had plenty of work on his plate if the sceptics and backstabbers were to be routed. 'You can't have your motor car, however top of the range, laid up in the garage for five years and expect to bring it out performing as new', reasoned some; 'Let's see him win a race he should have lost', demanded many more.

The first insider to raise his head above the parapet was Willie Carson. With his heart as ever worn boldly on his sleeve, the former champion, himself a bit of a veteran at 48, expressed grave misgivings about the wisdom of his one-time scourge attempting a comeback. In an interview for the *Daily Mirror* prior to the 1991 season he said: 'The legend is dead. Lester's an old man now – and he's looking it. It's sad but he's the forgotten man. I didn't think the comeback was a good idea. There's no way he could be the same. But it was heartening to see the old fellow walking back into the changing rooms.' Long gone were the days when Lester looked like he was part of a horse, Carson maintained; he's taken to riding longer so he could help his knees and legs; the mounts are not available; he's too old to be rushing up and down the country; and perhaps the unkindest cut of all: 'Even before his problems he wasn't riding all that well...he should see that he's had his career. It's over, even though the legend of his life will live on forever.' William Hill made Piggott a 50–1 no-hoper to win a 12th jockeys championship in 1991; anyone fancying his chances of a 30th Classic could get 6–1; those who foresaw a tenth Derby would be accommodated at 16–1.

However forlorn Lester's chances of achieving any of these targets, he picked up the gauntlet with almost tangible relish. Frequently to be seen on the Newmarket gallops of a morning, partnering one for Michael Stoute, Henry Cecil or Julie Cecil, in addition to those of his wife and son-in-law William Haggas, he converted the homework into early winners – nine by 2,000 Guineas day on May 4th. As if to emphasise the seriousness of his intentions he actually began his domestic campaign at Lingfield Park on one of the much-derided all-weather surfaces on March 23rd. Furthermore, he had even gone round to his next door neighbour, Ian Campbell to ask for the ride on First Stage in the 3.40.

Virtually to a man the top jockeys had studiously avoided the wintry delights offered by the 'sands' of Lingfield and Southwell. Piggott had not. He had already tested Southwell's fibresand on a chilly November afternoon at the back-end of 1990. 'I like the track very much', he said. 'It's surprisingly good. It's a fast track but it rides well. The kick-back is nothing really. It's better than racing on the American tracks because over there you do get kick-back that's bad but here it's nothing. The horses don't mind it.' Five rides, however, yielded nothing better than two seconds. Lingfield's equitrack proved more fruitful: a sparkling double on La Masaas and – surprise, surprise – the sought after First Stage. Piggott was pleased: 'I've enjoyed it here and although this is not such a galloping course as Southwell it rides well and all my mounts were happy on it. The sand comes up a bit, but nothing like it does in America and I wouldn't be at all worried about bringing a good horse here.'

Piggott's presence boosted the usually sparse all-weather crowds by 4–500. Southwell and Lingfield would not be alone in enjoying the benefits of racing's rejuvenated Pied Piper. Family and friends topped the list of beneficiaries. Having won for his wife in 1990, Piggott quickly proceeded to reward Julie Cecil and her mother, Lady Murless, as well as his son-in-law William Haggas. The success of Golan Heights in Newmarket's Remy Martin VSOP Cognac Handicap on April 18th was Julie Cecil's first as a trainer. 'I hope it's the first of many', said Piggott, whose initial encounter with Julie Cecil was in 1954 when he came to see her father Noel Murless about a job. 'She's seen so much of training horses, she's got to be good at it. I'd always hoped I would ride her first winner but I didn't think it would be today. Golan Heights has never done a great deal. Today he must have felt like it. Somebody must have told him that today was the day!' Piggott went on to complete a double on old pal Nicholas.

Two days later it was the turn of Lady Murless and William Haggas to profit from moments of Piggott magic. Down at Newbury, Lady Murless's St Ninian, trained by Peter Easterby, swept to an impressive four-length

The sweet smile of success: Bog Trotter has just won the Greenham to provide the first British Pattern race victory of the comeback *(Trevor Jones)*

victory in the Spring Cup, while the Haggas 3YO Bog Trotter received a tactical tour de force from Piggott in the Group III Greenham Stakes. Leading from the gate, Piggott kept just enough in reserve to withstand the late challenge ('Don't look round, daddy!' Maureen Haggas was yelling) of the favourite Mukaddamah, ridden by none other than the disparaging Willie Carson. 'Bog Trotter wants a fast pace and tucking-in', said the winning trainer. 'But how could I possibly give riding instructions to my father-in-law? All we said was "Good Afternoon"'. It had been another perfect day in a perfect week. 'Everything that could go right went right', said Lester. 'You couldn't ask for more, could you?'

'More' would be asked of Bog Trotter. Having won the Group II Champagne Stakes and been second in the Dewhurst as a 2YO, this Newbury success over the one-time 2,000 Guineas favourite confirmed Bog Trotter's right to be considered a worthy contender for the first colts' Classic – and with Piggott likely to ride his odds dropped from 20s to a best priced 12–1. 'I'm sure if Lester feels he can ride another horse he would ride it', Haggas admitted. 'When it comes down to it, he wants to win the race, it's as simple as that. I would not be offended.' Any threat to family harmony was averted: Piggott elected to ride Bog Trotter rather than Charles St George's Hokusai on whom he had finished third in the Craven Stakes to the new Guineas favourite Marju. Unfortunately, the family fortunes came unstuck. Piggott and Bog Trotter once again tried to make every yard but as the race began in earnest they rapidly back-pedalled and beat only two. 'He just dropped dead after leading. He stopped very quickly when he was squeezed out three from home.' Haggas subsequently provided the reason: 'He shouldn't have run. It was very naïve on my part. He'd had a temperature four days before and I thought I'd get away with it.'

The quest for Classic number 30 continued. Much to the media's glee that traditional annual guessing game of 'What will Lester ride in the Derby' could be revived and many column-inches safely filled in consequence.

In the three-and-a-half weeks leading up to the Derby on June 5th, Piggott's name was linked with no fewer than nine horses viz Corrupt (May 11); Peter Davies (May 15); Environment Friend (May 16); Sportsworld (May 21); Perpendicular (May 24); Hailsham and Peking Opera (May 27); Hector Protector (May 29); and Star of Gdansk (May 30). Some of the stories were wild rumours. Peter Davies, Sportsworld, Perpendicular and Peking Opera were all withdrawn; the connections of Corrupt, Environment Friend, Hector Protector and Star of Gdansk stuck by their jockeys – though in the case of Lingfield Derby Trial winner Corrupt, not without some loss of sleep. 'To be honest, I am in two minds. I am scared stiff to make the wrong decision', wailed the colt's owner Fathi Kalla. 'At the end of the day, it's all down to the horse. But Piggott is Piggott.' Kalla had clearly been listening to Vincent O'Brien.

With four days to go, Piggott still had no definite mount. Finally, on the Sunday before the Classic, the identity of Lester's 33rd Derby conveyance was revealed as Charles St George's 66–1 outsider Hokusai. 'It's well worth running: Lester needs the practice!' quipped the owner. Piggott responded: 'It will be a pleasure to ride in the Derby again, especially for Charles St George. Although Hokusai's odds suggest he doesn't have a leading chance, I'm hoping for the best. He has a better chance than people seem to believe. He's improving and I'm sure he stays the distance. We'll just have to wait and see what happens. It's nice to be involved in the Derby action again after so long and take another spin around the old place!'

News of the decision sparked off an immediate betting rush and Hokusai's odds were halved to 33s; Corals offered various novelty bets – 8–1 about Hokusai finishing in the first three; 5–1 to finish 4, 5 or 6; and 11–8 to finish 7, 8 or 9 of the 13 who went to post. No-hoper or not, the housewives and mug-punters would lump on Piggott. William Hill reported: 'We have been inundated with small bets, many from women. So far we stand to lose £$^1/_2$ million if he wins.' Corals said: 'If Lester wins we lose millions!'; the liability at Ladbrokes was around £5 million: 'That means £20 million around the country. We expect betting shops to become 'Piggott Banks' as millions of people have their annual flutter on their all-time favourite. This could be the worst day for the bookies since Red Rum won the 1974 National at 11–1'.

Lester's Lazarus-like participation in the Blue Riband raised the profile of a renewal that had a distinctly humdrum feel to it and gave the papers something to shout about on Derby day. 'Return of the Epsom magician' (*Daily Express*) and 'The King is Back' (*Daily Mirror*) typifying the headline writers' art. 'The King' attempted to explain how Derbies are won: 'There's no special trick. People talk about the difficulties of coming round Tattenham Corner: the truth is that it isn't that much of a problem. You have to place the horse, position is vital at every stage, but you have to keep coming back to the horse. What have you got, how does it respond, how does it act when you ask it to do something vital. The most important factor is acting on the course. If your horse doesn't handle the track, you're going to have problems coming down the hill. You just lose your place and it's hard to come back after'that. You cannot put the horse on one side. It begins and ends with them. Sure, the jockey is important but we shouldn't get carried away. If you have the right horse to act on the course and he has the speed to take up a good position, it's an easy race to ride in. It's what happens when you ask them to go and win the race that counts. When I go to Epsom for this Derby I won't be choking with emotion. I'll be seeing if we can get some kind of result.'

Piggott even got 'a result' in 1988 during his spell inside Highpoint by advising Kahyasi's rider Ray Cochrane how best to ride a Derby. 'Epsom is a real bitch of a course but Lester rides it brilliantly', said Cochrane. 'He is unique, the king round there. With all the twists and turns and gradients you have to be alert to problems every second. But Lester never makes mistakes. Basically, he's always in the right place at the right time.' Even Willie Carson was not ashamed to confess: 'The innate, the natural, horseman will always be able to give himself an extra chance in the Derby. I'm not a natural. None of us is. The only natural is Lester.'

Piggott's pre-race comments were graphically endorsed in the race itself. He had Hokusai perfectly positioned throughout the race (never worse than fourth) but when he asked the colt 'to go and win' nothing was forthcoming. 'I think I would have been third if he'd stayed but he didn't get the last furlong.' Hokusai finished seventh, a good 17 lengths

'The King is Back': Hokusai goes to post for Lester's 33rd Derby. *(Trevor Jones)*

behind the impressive winner, Generous. Nevertheless, Piggott had still played a part in victory: the successful jockey Alan Munro – on only his second Derby ride – had received personal instruction from the 'king' and had spent the previous evening in the company of Keith Piggott studying videos of Lester's nine triumphs. 'Lester's like a great big, thick book of knowledge', said Munro.

The towering significance of the Derby in Piggott's career meant that, in all honesty, it was good to have got the race out of the way: Hokusai had no realistic hope of victory, his sole purpose was to ensure that Hamlet was not performed without the Prince. The Oaks did pass minus Piggott but the St Leger (in which he required one more victory to equal William Scott's 145 year-old record of nine) would not be so deprived. Besides training Hokusai for St George, Henry Cecil also handled a 3YO half brother to the owner's 1989 St Leger winner Michelozzo called Micheletti. So immature that he did not see a racetrack until the July of his third year, Micheletti proved himself a progressive sort of colt. After winning his Leicester maiden he added a minor conditions race at Newmarket before landing the £16,570 Melrose Handicap over $1^3/_4$ miles at the big York August meeting, a race occasionally used as a stepping stone to the St Leger by an improving 3YO. 'He could be a Leger horse', mused Piggott. 'He stays well but it will all depend on what is left in the race.' For his part, St George joked: 'Do you think my jockey will get the trip?' Lester's 26th and most recent Leger mount had been St George's Lanfranco, third to Oh So Sharp in 1985. On September 4th Micheletti was confirmed as ride number 27.

As so often in modern times, the final Classic cut up into a small, comparatively undistinguished field which prompted all the usual cries from the revisionists exhorting the authorities to tinker with its conditions: reduce the distance; open the race to all ages. Piggott staunchly upheld the traditionalist viewpoint: 'They should leave the Leger as it is. It is still a great race and always will be and it takes a good horse to win it. People only knock it because of the distance but that's ridiculous. We still need this type of race. Quite honestly, if we had all our good races at $1\frac{1}{2}$ miles or less like the Americans it would be very boring.' And the possibility of Micheletti being 'a really good horse'? 'Timeform say I've got no chance but the race has been lucky for me. Micheletti's improving. We don't know whether he's good enough, really. His form comes up 7-10lb behind the two favourites but we're hoping for the best. He's got a bit to find because he's come from a handicap and he's only had three races but he seems to stay all right and that's the big thing here. I've got to be optimistic.'

Although backed down to 6–1 second favourite, Micheletti, as Piggott feared, lacked the class of proven Pattern race performers like Toulon (the 5–2 favourite) and Saddler's Hall, finishing a well-beaten third in a very fast race. 'It was a tough race, better than it looked on paper, and my horse was beaten by experience. He is still a bit immature and green.'

Lester may have failed in the final Classic but he managed to light up Town Moor with three displays of absolute pyrotechnics during the four-day St Leger meeting aboard Bog Trotter, Mudaffar and You Know The Rules. 'Lester calls the shots', declared the *Racing Post* in the afterglow of Friday's double initiated on the front-running Bog Trotter in the Group III Kiveton Park Stakes and completed by the fast-finishing Mudaffar, trained by brother-in-law, Robert Armstrong, in the People-Sporting Life Handicap. Pat Eddery looked to have the handicap well sewn up on Troupe as he entered the final furlong. 'They went quite fast and the first two horses were the last two into the straight', Piggott explained to Channel 4 viewers. 'Pat went through them very easily and I was following him. When he came past me he had a good look at me and had a little laugh. But when he got to the front his horse stopped a little and I was really coming over the last furlong. Pat's horse just went up and down

Making Sirrell Griffith's day by riding his Cheltenham Gold Cup winner Norton's Coin in the 1991 Queen Alexandra *(John Crofts)*

in the same spot.' As Troupe and Mudaffar flashed past the post, Piggott glanced across at Eddery. No words were said: the look was sufficient. Then, on the Saturday, an hour after the St Leger, Lester produced a carbon copy of the ride on Mudaffar to force You Know The Rules up on the line to short head Silver Braid for the Reference Point Sceptre Stakes.

Owners, trainers, punters and Piggott pilgrims the length and breadth of Britain were treated to vignettes like these throughout the Second Coming, but particularly in 1991 and 1992. At Newbury in May 1991 Piggott used his vast knowledge of the track to snatch the Group II Lockinge Stakes out of the fire; he knew from experience that when the ground in Newbury's straight was heavy, the stands side invariably rode slightly better. The 2–1 on favourite In The Groove and the other two runners crawled up the middle for the first three-quarters of the one mile contest: Piggott, meanwhile, loitered in the rear on Polar Falcon until the closing stages, whereupon he brought the French colt with a wet sail up the stands' fence to upset the favourite by two lengths.

The scene-stealing act then shifted to Ascot and his 115th winner at the Royal meeting. 'Lester dazzles Royal Ascot: Piggott makes it just like old days', opined *The Sporting Life* after the 18-times leading jockey at the prestigious fixture ('There's nothing like it. It's the best meeting of the year') gave a masterly exhibition of tactics on Saddler's Hall in the Group II King Edward VII Stakes. 'I'll not be doing any hanging about', Piggott assured trainer Michael Stoute in the paddock beforehand, and true to his word, as soon as the stalls opened he took the race by the scruff of the neck. Thereafter, an injection of pace on the bend killed off any potential danger, leaving Saddler's Hall to romp home by six lengths. 'At York I should have been closer with him', Piggott told the press, referring to the defeat Saddler's Hall suffered last time out. 'It was a slow race and he was a bit green. Today nobody wanted to go on. I was quite happy being up there. I've ridden the horse in work all year. He's a very nice horse – he's just taken a bit of time to show what he can do.'

Royal Ascot 1991 also provided a wonderful illustration of Piggott's cult status among the 'little men' of the training fraternity, when he agreed to partner the 1990 Cheltenham Gold Cup winner Norton's Coin for Carmarthen dairy farmer Sirrell Griffiths in the Queen Alexandra Stakes. 'To sit in the stands at Royal Ascot watching my horse canter to the start with Lester Piggott on board would be the thrill of a lifetime', said Griffiths. 'I have always been a great fan of his. Lester is simply the best there is. I used to follow Flat racing very closely but when Lester retired I lost interest.' A racecourse gallop at Newbury on the 10YO gelding was enough to persuade Piggott to accept the mount. This particular pipe dream fizzled out: Norton's Coin finished 9th of 13. However, several other owners and trainers who sought Lester's services on a one-off basis went away with moments to treasure. In 1991, for example, Piggott rode

Saddler's Hall makes it 115 winners at Royal Ascot *(Trevor Jones)*

for 85 different trainers with 41 of them providing just a single mount; in 1992 the respective figures were 74/34; followed by 70/32 (1993) and 58/22 (1994). To put the great man up on a winner was a real red-letter day in the lives of many a trainer.

Jack Berry (Bit-A-Magic: Folkestone, May 20th, 1991): 'He has ridden for us before but had not previously been successful. He only came back so that he could ride a winner for us!'

James Eustace (Master of Passion: Leicester, May 28th, 1991): 'I realised Lester knew the horse's owner and thought he might do the trick, so I asked him to ride work on the horse. The work went well; Lester just grunted, "He's all right." And the horse duly scooted in!'

Lord John Fitzgerald (Songster: Leicester, September 10th, 1991): 'Lester retired at just the point when I started training which meant that I was never able to have him ride one for me. Since he came back I haven't had the horses that I could put him on but I thought this one would suit him.'

Simon Dow (Itsagame: Goodwood, August 1st, 1991): 'This was his first ride for me. It's like a schoolboy ambition I've had since I was 16. He's superlative, in a class of his own. I had suggested to him – how can I give him orders? – that the best idea might be to 'tuck him in' but his idea seemed very much more to drop Itsagame out!'

Ben Hanbury (Burdur: Epsom, June 6th, 1991): 'Lester's been asking me for rides but I told him I wasn't going to put him up unless we had a good chance of winning. We've backed this one well at 10-1!'

Eric Wheeler (Green Dollar: Epsom, June 7th, 1991): 'I rang up Lester – you don't expect God to ring you! It's the first time he has ridden for me and I apologised in the paddock for the fact that it was raining!'

Eddie Harty (Sha's Dream: Curragh, August 17th, 1991): 'For 20 years I've been trying to get him to ride one of mine. When I was in England his parents were very good to me and we've been friends for years.'

Jon Scargill (Snowy River: Nottingham, September 22nd, 1992): 'This was his debut for me. When I rang him up there was a lot of thumbing through the formbook before he said yes. It would have been impertinent of me to give him orders but as a football manager might say: "The boy Piggott done good!"'

Alan Bailey (Never So Sure: York, September 2nd, 1992): 'I have always wanted a winner at York. Lester said we should put the visor on instead of blinkers; he said the horse had not seen the other two coming when they got beat at Goodwood, so we put the visor on so he could see a bit more if necessary. It is no good paying him if you are not going to listen to him. There is only one authority higher than Lester – and he is in heaven!'

And owners too.

George Cole (Huso: Nottingham, May 31st, 1991): 'I'd never spoken to Lester before today and even meeting him has been a great thrill. He gave Huso a great ride, but then he would, wouldn't he?'

David Faulkner (Eager Deva: Pontefract: May 4th, 1992): 'Lester rode Continhugh at Ascot for me back in the 70s. He was a decent horse who'd finished fourth in the Gimcrack but he was beaten about two furlongs and I was almost ashamed to go and talk to Lester afterwards. But when I met him Lester said not to worry and that he'd win next time out. He did, too, at Newcastle by six lengths!'

Quite a few courses were also in for a treat. 'Funny, but you forget about tracks. You have to go back and remember the best place to go, where the ground is. You've got to be a bit sharp to remember 40 tracks!'

Some courses made greater demands upon Piggott's memory than others. In May 1993, he went to Bath for the first time in 22 years and won on the Queen's Desert Love; a year later he went one better by riding a winner at Carlisle (Mazeeka), a venue unfrequented since 1966. 'Nothing much has changed since I was last here! But it is a lovely little track and it is good to come back here though the ground is rock hard.'

More conventional treats, in the form of trebles, were enjoyed by the clientele at Leicester (July 16th, 1991) and Kempton Park (May 3rd, 1993); and it was at Leicester in October 1991 that he celebrated the first anniversary of his memorable return with a success on Claret, the 102nd winner of the 12 months. The 100th was brought up at the Curragh on October 13th by Colway Bold in the £140,000 Goffs Premier Challenge, one of the biggest prizes in Piggott's entire career.

'The year has flown by. I'm enjoying it. I wouldn't be doing it otherwise. I don't hurry about too much – I've probably only ridden four days a week so it's quite easy. And I would have to say that it has worked out much better than I could have hoped. It's really been a lot of fun and just like old times. I really never thought I would have had so many rides. I'm lighter than I was before. Some people get lighter as they get older and I'm definitely lighter than I was. I'm just not a big eater. Doesn't bother me, eating. You've got to keep yourself fit all the time. Very hard but it's no bad thing. If I let myself go, my weight would go way over 8st 6lb and I'd be no use to anyone. My problem is everyone thinks I'm too old. I can't retire again, can I? I've done that once. So I'll just have to win a few races. All I want to do is get out there and ride horses because that's what I do best. Some people think I'm mad to be like this at my age – maybe they're right! I haven't really stopped since I started and the more you ride the better for you. I think you see what is going to happen before it happens. It's marvellous to be wanted. I always had a big following. The English racing public didn't forget me. They sent me a lot of letters, lovely letters. All of a sudden I was back. And I realised how much I'd missed it.'

Needless to say, Piggott's outrageously successful return ensured a shower of awards. In March 1991 he was the recipient of a Special Award for services to racing at the William Hill Golden Spurs lunch, and later the same month he took the Sportsperson of the Year prize at the inaugural Jockeys Association Awards – awards that were quickly christened 'Lesters'. Twelve months on he won the latter once again ('The only thing I thought I'd be coming up here to collect would be my old age pension') and at the end of 1992 he also scooped the Cartier Award of Merit for the year's outstanding contribution to European racing. A hat-trick of 'Lester's' proved a mere formality and he strode on stage at the London Hilton to collect the trophy on Sunday, March 28th, 1993, with the words of Tina Turner's *Simply the Best* ringing in his ears.

Piggott would never again be champion jockey: the bookmakers were right about that. But what about a 30th English Classic? All he needed was one last good horse.

5

THE LAST GOOD HORSE

Whenever the great races came round, particularly the Classics, and most pointedly the Derby, Robert Sangster would always recall Vincent O'Brien's credo: 'The great joy of having Lester on your horse was that he wasn't riding someone else's.' In three seasons at the end of the 1970s Piggott had won Sangster a brace of Arcs (on Alleged), a Derby, Irish Derby and a King George (on The Minstrel), the Irish 1,000 Guineas and Oaks (Godetia) and the Irish 2,000 Guineas (Jaazeiro) – not to mention a host of other Group Is. Sangster's luck, though hardly wretched, was not always subsequently so uniformly rich. After El Gran Senor had lost the 1984 Derby by a short head in the hands of Pat Eddery the owner was passed by Piggott: 'Missing me?' was the ensuing phrase that has entered racing folklore. In the spring of 1992 Sangster had a Classic contender in Rodrigo de Triano. However, as the 2,000 Guineas approached he had no jockey.

Named after the lookout (though misspelt: it should be Triana) on Columbus's *Santa Maria* who reputedly first spotted landfall across the Atlantic in 1492, the chestnut son of El Gran Senor was regarded the best English-trained colt of his generation at two as a consequence of winning all his five races, which included the Group II Champagne and the Group I Middle Park. Only the French superstar Arazi was rated his superior and Arazi, at the behest of his American owner, was being aimed at the Kentucky Derby, run on the same day as the 2,000 Guineas. There is no 'sure thing' in racing but with normal progress through the winter Rodrigo's chances in the Guineas were plainly evident.

At Doncaster and Newmarket, Rodrigo had the assistance of Willie Carson and it was with Carson in the saddle that Rodrigo was a well-beaten fourth (to Lion Cavern, whom he had defeated in the Middle Park) in his 2,000 Guineas prep race, Newbury's Greenham Stakes on April 11th. However, Carson was sure to be claimed by Sheikh Hamdan al

Another fruitful partnership is revived: Piggott and Sangster plot the future
(Trevor Jones)

Maktoum for one of his two representatives in the first Classic. Surprisingly, it proved to be Rodrigo's trainer not owner who suggested Piggott be offered the mount: surprising because 29 year-old Peter Chapple-Hyam had only been training for one season and the owner he was advising happened to be both his step father-in-law and his landlord. 'It was my idea for Lester to ride. Lester's simply the best when it comes to the big races. I felt Rodrigo would suit Lester really well and it couldn't have worked out better as they got on like Torvill and Dean. Rodrigo was not an easy ride in that he tended to pull himself up when he hit the front; he had to be dropped out and brought with a late run. Lester was the ideal jockey for him because he'd sit and wait.'

One of Sangster's favourite sayings is: 'Life is all about timing.' Chapple-Hyam had timed things just nicely. Having had next-to-no racing background until he joined Barry Hills as an 18 year-old pupil assistant in 1981, his elevation to the custodianship of Sangster's custom-built 2,300 acre training centre at Manton was to many cynical outsiders a wonderful instance of the old Hollywood cliche 'the son-in-law also rises'. Chapple-Hyam came to Manton as one of Hills' assistant trainers in 1987; three years later he married Sangster's step-daughter and when Hills left Manton at the end of 1990 (having failed to raise the capital to buy the estate and convert it into a multi-trainer complex) Sangster put Chapple-Hyam in charge. The young novice did not disappoint his patron: 27 victories in 1991 included the Group I Dewhurst from Dr Devious in addition to Rodrigo's Middle Park.

'How could I have the luck to come up with him', said Sangster. 'He just seems to make such sense of it all. I have known many great trainers and he could be a match for any of them. When we knew Willie Carson wasn't going to be available we looked at Cash Asmussen and Frankie Dettori but thought Lester would be the best at getting Rodrigo to settle.' The booking was confirmed on April 21st and the bookmakers reacted immediately by shortening Rodrigo's price to 4–1. The colt – known around the yard as Rodney or The Plonker after the character in the hit TV comedy *Only Fools and Horses* – had thrived since his Greenham defeat. 'Rodrigo grew three inches in the winter and got a lot stronger. He was some 30 kilos heavier in the Greenham than when he won the Middle Park, which is a lot, even allowing for a horse strengthening between two and three and putting on weight over the winter. When I weighed him a week before he was actually 37 kilos over and I was nearly panicking. But I didn't want to rush him. The idea was to take him to Newbury needing the run; I wasn't disappointed at all. He was bang there looking the winner two out until he just blew up on the soft ground, which he hated. I blame myself for what happened but there was no point leaving the Guineas behind in the Greenham.'

A week that could develop into the greatest of Chapple-Hyam's life opened with him feeling distinctly upbeat. His horses were in fine form; he had fancied runners in both the Guineas and Kentucky Derby in Rodrigo and the now American-owned Dr Devious; but then Rodrigo got a sore heel and trotted lame, the infection went up his tendon. Laser and poultice treatment cleared up the problem within days and Rodrigo was soon cantering again. 'There was nothing too serious to worry about. It was really only a small infection but at this stage of the proceedings you could do without annoying hiccups like that. I must admit the pressure got to me. It brought on a bout of flu and I went to bed!'

Chapple-Hyam was not sure if his nerves would be strong enough to withstand the strain: the Guineas *and* Kentucky Derby to worry about. Some pundits questioned the wisdom of entrusting the English leg of the double to Piggott. He had ridden, it was pointed out, only 37 races in the domestic season and just the one winner; during Channel 4's *Morning Line* programme on raceday itself John McCririck was adamant the decision to put up Piggott was a mistake; and, in *The Sun*, Willie Carson was quoted as saying: 'We used to call him "God" but not at 56. He's lucky to be able to get out of his armchair let alone ride Classic winners'.

The saddlecloth says it all: Numero Uno is back *(Trevor Jones)*

An ecstatic Jacqueline O'Brien greets Royal Academy after the Breeders' Cup Mile
(*Trevor Jones*)

The big grey, El Prado: 'He's not as dedicated as you or I,' Lester informs O'Brien
(*Trevor Jones*)

The Last Hurrah for the Old Firm: Vincent O'Brien leads in the victorious Piggott and College Chapel after the Cork & Orrery at Royal Ascot on June 17,1993 *(John Crofts)*

Welcome to the world of advertising! *(Racing Post)*

At full stretch on Bog Trotter, trained by son-in-law William Haggas *(Trevor Jones)*

Thanks! Rodrigo de Triano has just provided victory in a 30th English Classic *(John Crofts)*

Right: The 4493rd and final winner on the Flat in Britain: the grey Palacegate Jack gets up to win the King's Regiment Cup at Haydock Park on October 5 1994
(Colin Turner)

Below: All the old 'Piggott Power' is summoned up to get Fylde Flyer (far side) home in the 1992 Abernant Stakes at Newmarket
(John Crofts)

Left: Minutes from disaster: Lester and Mr Brooks parade in front of the stands before the Breeders' Cup Sprint at Gulfstream Park on October 31, 1992
(Trevor Jones)

Right: Flanked by Roy Miller's two paintings which were to be mounted on The Piggott Gates at Epsom
(Racing Post)

Once more in the colours of his monarch: is it still possible Her Majesty might one day say 'Arise, Sir Lester'? *(John Crofts)*

English Classic number 30 is in the bag *(Trevor Jones)*

Fate decreed otherwise. It was, after all, the 500th anniversary of Rodrigo's namesake staking his claim to immortal fame; Rodrigo was the youngest horse in the race (his third birthday was not till May 27th) with the youngest trainer and the oldest jockey. The result was foretold in the stars; all Lester Piggott had to do was reach for the rewind button. The banner headlines had to be read to verify the evidence of our own disbelieving eyes: 'Piggott turns back the clock' (*Sunday Times* and *Sporting Life*); 'He's just incredible!' (*Racing Post*); 'Vintage Lester' (*Mail on Sunday*); 'Piggott's timeless Classic touch' (*Independent on Sunday*); 'The Greatest Grandfather' (*Daily Mail*).

Between the showers of a blustery afternoon, Newmarket Heath was illuminated by a shaft of the old conjurer's brightest sunshine. As the leading bunch chopped and changed positions through torrid early quarters, expending all manner of energy in the process, Piggott, who had broken slowly from his stall three off the fence, tacked to the centre of the track to occupy a position between the two emerging groups. In so doing he avoided all the hustle and bustle which ultimately ensued toward the inside. This intuitive tactical coup, ranking alongside any of his previous 29 Classic-winning manoeuvres, made number 30 an indecent formality. This was not, it's true, the renowned cold-eyed gunslinging style of yesteryear; the 'most famous shootist extant' calling out his hapless victim with sadistic relish. This was more the silver-haired, card-sharping riverboat gambler with an ace up each sleeve waiting to be slipped into play when the game demanded. Exploiting his wonderfully trouble-free passage to the hilt, Piggott delivered Rodrigo's challenge entering the Dip to win going away by one-and-a-half lengths from Lucky Lindy.

The first of those 30 English Classics had come way back in the Derby of 1954 on Never Say Die; the most recent in the 2,000 Guineas on Shadeed almost seven years ago to the day. 'Lester may be a grandfather but he's still the best, isn't he?' enthused a jubilant Chapple-Hyam. 'Of course I wasn't worried about putting him up. He's as good as ever. He was riding winners before I was born. He came to ride Rodrigo at Manton and although he didn't say much you could tell he was a bit excited. I told him to sit and wait and not hit the front too soon and his words to me were: "They won't see me coming!"' Robert Sangster had difficulty containing his delight; not just because this was his first Classic in six years, but because of his trainer and jockey. 'They have made a great team, the youngest trainer and the oldest jockey! I am absolutely delighted for them. I told Lester to just sit and relax and enjoy himself. I always thought he was the right man for the horse. He would settle the colt and get him switched off. I think this has to be the best of my Classic wins. It is the first we have had from Manton and both the sire and dam carried my colours – and with Peter training the colt and Lester, who has been a great pal for years, riding him it was the perfect result.'

Old Stoneface was again belying this increasingly redundant soubriquet: his face resembled a walnut about to self-combust as he cut a swathe through all the back-slapping for what amounted to a reprise of his Belmont interview with Brough Scott. 'They went a bit faster than I thought they would, I didn't see what was likely to make it and I was back a bit. But I was comfortable enough. I had a good run through the middle and once I got to the Bushes I knew I was going to win anyway. Everyone was frightened he wouldn't get the trip; I always thought he would. He was always going so easily that he would have won even if he hadn't stayed the distance. I think he is a very good winner. He quickened very well when I asked him. He as the best 2YO last year after all. I'm lucky: I've always stayed fit and today I was lucky to be on the right horse. This win means an awful lot to me.' Scott could not avoid finishing with: 'So, there you are, Lester, a 56 year-old grandfather. You shouldn't be out doing this!' The old gunslinger was waiting for him: 'You mustn't keep telling everyone that!' Scott tried again: 'How long can it go on?' Now the card-sharp materialised to scoop the pot: 'I'll get to the fifth race anyway!'

The logical next step for Rodrigo de Triano was the Irish 2,000 Guineas a fortnight later. The task, on the face of it, was not a taxing one and

Piggott's 16th Irish Classic already seemed rubber-stamped. Only five opposed, headed by Lucky Lindy and Ezzoud, a short head second to the Guineas runner up at Kempton. Rodrigo became the fourth horse to achieve the Guineas double just like an 11–8 favourite should. Settled last for most of the race while Irish Memory and Lucky Lindy disputed the lead, he literally cantered over his rivals. However, as everyone geared themselves for the sight of a majestic sweep round the outside Piggott, as usual, took the less obvious route.

'When he was still last after the two furlong marker', Chapple-Hyam later confessed, 'I said to myself "Why doesn't he come on the outside?". When I next saw him he was in front and the race was over!' As soon as a gap had appeared between the weakening pair up front Piggott instinctively shot Rodrigo through it on the diagonal, in a sudden dive for the rail. 'Clearly Lester isn't as fit as he was 20 years ago: he couldn't possibly be', continued Chapple-Hyam. 'But what a brain! When it comes to raceriding he has the best mind in the business.' Piggott's elan put the seal of a maestro on what could have been a mere run-of-the-mill success and the Irish crowd responded in kind. 'If Lester were to break into song', said Ted Walsh on RTE, 'they couldn't greet him any warmer than that.'

Another Sangster-Piggott assault on the Derby – initially ruled out after the English Guineas – had now moved to the forefront of Sangster's mind: 'One should be allowed time to reflect and it would be unfair to expect us to commit ourselves to Epsom now. I wouldn't run Rodrigo for the sake of running. He'd have to go with a 6–1 chance. Sentiment says it would be great to have Lester riding a horse in the Derby with a very, very live 6 or 7–1 chance. As sport that would be great. As a practical man I would say Rodrigo wouldn't stay. Logic and breeding dictates that we should stick to a mile. But as sport I'd have him running.'

Racing opinion was split down the middle. With no outstanding middle-distance colt dominating the picture it was worth giving Rodrigo a shot, ran one argument: against that the breeding pundits insisted he had no earthly chance of staying the $1\frac{1}{2}$ miles being out of a sprint-bred mare. The bookmakers did not know what to do. William Hill made Rodrigo a skinny 4–1 joint favourite while Corals and Ladbrokes went 10s.

Back in 1977, Piggott had solved Sangster's dilemma concerning The Minstrel's Derby participation following defeats in the English and Irish Guineas: 'You run him and I'll ride him', Lester said then; he was less certain this time round.

The final decision rested with Chapple-Hyam, who kept up an almost continuous dialogue with the press. 'Lester is not as keen as I am about Rodrigo getting the trip but of course he will have first refusal on the mount at Epsom. Who else would I want on board? He would kill me if I didn't give him the ride. Obviously, I shall be talking to Robert Sangster about Epsom but he is very keen to run as well. Rodrigo has improved 7lb since Newmarket and the way he has been working is fantastic. We had to rush his preparation for Newmarket but we were able to train him properly for the Irish Guineas. Quietly, on the way back, Lester told me that Rodrigo de Triano is as good a horse as he's ever ridden – and he will improve again on faster ground. Over a mile he is the best but if he doesn't get the $1^1/_2$ miles in the Derby he loses nothing and we can go back to a mile. Whether or not he runs in the Derby is ultimately my decision.'

As the days were ticked off the calendar, Chapple-Hyam's apprehension began to lift. Rodrigo worked well over ten furlongs; the opposition was weak; most of the leading contenders were bred for speed and had the same question marks against their stamina as Rodrigo; the second favourite was his own Dr Devious, not seen in public since finishing seventh in the Kentucky Derby. What was there to lose? A faint heart never won anything. Accordingly, his patron's 'sporting' option rapidly developed into a 'practical' proposition. 'Either he is going to stay or he's not! But I'm getting more confident by the day watching him settling so well and being so relaxed. Lester told me that he thinks he is as good as Sir Ivor and he is planning to ride him in a similar way. He said he will send me a tape of how he did it. But I hope he does not leave it too late – my heart wouldn't stand it! If Rodrigo and the 'Doctor' enter the final furlong locked together I think Rodrigo will win as he's got so much class. But really I won't mind too much as long as one of them wins!'

Chapple-Hyam got his wish. Victory in the 213th Derby went to Manton: but it was Dr Devious not Rodrigo de Triano who made him the youngest ever Derby-winning trainer. The *Racing Post* had posed the question: 'Can he do it?' The paper was, of course, referring to Lester Piggott rather than his mount. Inside, Paul Haigh wrote comically: 'One of the problems of Piggottolatry (or dementia lesterensis as it is known in the psychiatric profession) is the irrational belief that whatever Lester Piggott rides will win the Derby.' Likely victims, Haigh continued, were often recognisable by 'glazed eyes, curlers, fag in the corner of the mouth and a tendency to hum the tune from *Neighbours*'. The *cognoscenti* said Piggott and Rodrigo hadn't a prayer: the rest of Britain prayed that they did. Not even an inch of rain during Derby week ('If I didn't run him', said his beleaguered trainer, 'I think they would hang me from the top of that flagpole on the grandstand.') which left the last vital three furlongs in the straight good – soft could stop the disease from spreading like wild fire. Betting shop money ensured Rodrigo de Triano was sent off the 13–2 favourite. 'It's basically all about the Piggott factor', said Ladbroke's Mike Dillon aping his comments of 1991. 'And if they win the betting industry will pay out something in the region of £20 million.'

Piggott's public never got a run for their money. Lester rode Rodrigo as one knew he must: from the back. Descending Tattenham hill he had only five horses behind him and, ominously, was already losing touch with the pack. Nevertheless, Lester did not set about Rodrigo in an attempt to put him in the race. 'He just did not handle the course and didn't stay. We never got nearer than at the finish', was the all-embracing, succinct as ever, Piggott post mortem. They finished ninth. Only the bookies had reason to be cheerful. 'If Rodrigo had won we would have been paying out till midnight', said Don Payne of William Hill. Whether the favourite's demise was caused by lack of stamina, an inability to cope with the track or the pressure of the parade (there was so much cheering for Lester that Rodrigo's eyes were popping out of his head) – or a combination of all three – Rodrigo de Triano was not given a hard race. Plan A had failed; it was time for Plan B to be put into operation.

At the close of the 1991 season, Chapple-Hyam had received a fair amount of flak for suggesting that Rodrigo was a better horse than Arazi, the winner of three Group I events in France before crossing the Atlantic to stun the Americans with a truly awesome five length victory in the Breeders' Cup Juvenile over 8 $\frac{1}{2}$ furlongs at Churchill Downs. Arazi's assault on the 1$\frac{1}{4}$ miles Kentucky Derby proved a dismal failure; after looking dangerous on the final turn he faded into eighth, one place behind Dr Devious. Now, Chapple-Hyam was itching to take on the fallen French superstar over a mile with his very own. 'If he doesn't come to England I shall go to France to find him!'

The showdown materialised sooner than expected: the St James's Palace Stakes at Royal Ascot – just 13 days after the Derby. Rodrigo reportedly lost 18 kilos – 'about 8 kilos too much' – in the Derby but was soon back to his optimum racing weight and although Chapple-Hyam admitted another week's respite was preferable, the die was cast. 'Mr Sangster is a sportsman and not one to shirk a challenge. If we had backed out of this one it would have been very easy for everyone to have had a go at us, but we're happy to take Arazi on. Rodrigo was at his best before the

Irish Guineas and comparing him with how he was at the Curragh, he is not quite spot on. Lester is going to sit, wait and pounce. I don't mind what the others do. They can go as fast as they like or as slow as they like. But you won't see us until as late as possible. If Rodrigo hadn't run in the Derby I would have been very keen indeed.'

What was billed variously as the 'Royal Rumble' (*Racing Post*) and the 'Coe – Ovett showdown of the Turf' (*Daily Mail*) turned out to be a damp squib. In an eight-horse field, Arazi (11–10 on), who had only recently resumed full work, and Rodrigo (4–1) played cat and mouse in rear until meeting the straight, where both challenged on the wide outside. Arazi got first run without ever looking likely to collect the leaders – Zaahi and Ezzoud, on the rail – before Lester produced Rodrigo even wider out. Rodrigo won their private duel but the 25–1 Irish colt Brief Truce won the race, getting up in the last stride to pip Zaahi. 'Giants reveal feet of clay', was the *Post*'s damning headline; 'Ascot anti-climax as Irish outsider eclipses titans', said the *Daily Telegraph*. Piggott was never one to be fazed. 'He wasn't quite the horse he was before the Derby. He wasn't going well on the turn into the straight. I'm sure he'll come back. Let's face it, I beat the Wonder Horse!' Rodrigo plainly wanted a rest: in the Irish 2,000 Guineas he had humiliated Brief Truce and Ezzoud.

The rematch between Rodrigo and Arazi with the mile championship of Europe at stake never came off. Somewhat surprisingly, in fact, Rodrigo de Triano never again ran over the distance. It was intended he should return to action in Deauville's one mile Prix Jacques le Marois on August 16th but unsuitable heavy ground caused him to be rerouted to York for the Juddmonte International over an extended ten furlongs. Warm favourite in a very competitive field was the Irish filly Kooyonga, winner of the Eclipse; also in the line-up were four other Group I winners (including Dr Devious) plus the Oaks runner-up All At Sea. 'Kooyonga may be in for a shock', teased Chapple-Hyam. 'The International is famous for the shock results it has thrown up.' He neglected to say which of the Manton duo would cause the shock, though he did give a pointer by revealing Dr Devious might just be a couple of gallops short. Rodrigo, on the other hand, was clearly jumping out of his skin. Chapple-Hyam thought it might be a good idea for Piggott to go down to Manton and ride the colt in a $1\frac{1}{4}$ mile gallop round a bend in preparation for York. Relentless Pursuit led a quartet completed by Rodrigo, Dr Devious and Corrupt, a recent acquisition to the stable who was being aimed at a Group III race on the same Deauville card as the Jacques le Marois. 'Rodrigo came past me at the top of the gallop going like Pegasus! He was about 20 lengths clear of Dr Devious, who was a similar distance in front of Corrupt. He went out the top of the gallop and through the gate still going so strongly that Lester had to aim him at quite a high barbed-wire fence in order to stop him. I don't mind admitting I nearly died! When I eventually caught up with them I was virtually tearing my hair out but I was relieved to find that Rodrigo was unmarked and Lester had a big grin on his face. He turned to me and all he said was: "If you'd got him this ready for the Guineas I wouldn't have had to have moved!"' All that needs to be added is that on the Sunday before the International, Corrupt won his Group III with something to spare.

In a race run at a blistering gallop, Piggott brought Rodrigo (8–1 at the off) through from the back in a carbon copy of Royal Academy's Breeders' Cup to once again bring the house down. The *Daily Mail*'s 'Piggott, the grand old Duke of York' headline was not far off the mark because his reception upon entering the winner's enclosure would have flattered any visiting aristocrat. Chapple-Hyam engulfed his jockey in a huge bear-hug before gushing: 'This is the greatest day of my racing life. It means more than winning the Derby. So many people have rubbished Rodrigo and said he wouldn't stay. But he's proved what I always thought: he's a real race horse. The best in Europe. How many horses win Group Is over six furlongs, a mile and ten furlongs? This fellow is exceptional.'

Robert Sangster also found it a struggle to keep his emotions in check: 'I've had 105 Group I winners and have no hesitation in nominating this one as giving me the most satisfaction. He's home-bred; it's Lester; and it's the International at York. Lester is a folk hero at York and I've never heard applause like that before. When I arrived at the track the first person I saw was Lester getting out of a taxi and they always say back the first jockey you meet! I thought he was going to tap me for the fare but, incredibly, Lester asked me what to do in the race! He was anxious because he was drawn right on the outside. It's the first time I can remember in 25 years that he has asked me what he should do in a race. I said do the same as you did in the Derby – drop him out and come from behind.'

Piggott's task was made considerably more straightforward by Alnasr Alwasheek, who dragged the runners to the two furlong pole faster than the equivalent fraction in the track record International of 1988. As those ridden close to this severe pace wilted, the patiently-ridden Rodrigo de Triano, to use Piggott's own term, 'glided' through from the back to beat All At Sea by a length. Rodrigo may have given the impression of superb acceleration but in actual fact the final quarter was the slowest of the race. His success owed more to the superb jockeyship of the wily and wizened

'Oh no! Not bloody Lester again!': the Champion Stakes is won *(John Crofts)*

character on his back, the 'Great Antiquity' as Paul Haigh had lately christened him. 'Rodrigo showstopper' and 'Peerless Piggott' was how the
sport's two trade papers chose to sum up the outcome of the 1992
International. It was impossible to argue.

On October 17th, Rodrigo de Triano went for his fifth
consecutiveGroup I contest, the Champion Stakes, worth £216,176, over
1¼ miles at Newmarket. The colt's preparation had left much to be
desired; a recurring splint on his off-fore meant more sleepless nights for
Chapple-Hyam and Rodrigo came to Newmarket largely on a training
regime of walking, swimming and cantering. 'We would probably run
him on two legs if we had to', said Sangster, tongue planted firmly in
cheek. 'Hopefully, we should win it even he is threequarters fit.'

With the horse still lame on the Thursday, Chapple-Hyam took the
unorthodox step of galloping him a full mile 24 hours before the race.
Rodrigo passed the fitness test but as he circled the Newmarket paddock
the unaccustomed sight of bandages on his forelegs confirmed how
touch and go his presence in the field had been. However, no longer
surrounded by stamina doubts and enjoying the luxury of his preferred
good-firm ground, Rodrigo de Triano was backed from 2–1 to 11–8

favourite to beat Lahib (who had opened favourite) and eight others. The result was never in question once Zaahi began to set a fast pace on behalf of Lahib. As usual, Piggott ignored the pacesetters and ran the race at his own pace, the pace which suited *his* horse. Such tactics demand tremendous mental courage: 'bottle', in modern sporting parlance. Piggott sat still and stayed that way for as long as he dare. No need to kick and shove for ten furlongs, just keeping his powder dry for when it really mattered. He tracked Willie Carson on Lahib, followed him through and past the pacemaker running into the Dip and pounced up the hill to win, hands and heels, by a neck.

'I just wish Rodrigo's splint had been a bit bigger', joked Carson. 'I saw Rodrigo coming and I thought: 'Oh no! Not bloody Lester again!' Piggott was quick to pay tribute to his partner: 'Rodrigo is a racing machine. You only have to look at his record to see that he is a great horse. He's been on the go since the spring and he's won four Group Is. He must rate with the best of any generation. He is among the best I've ridden; he compares very favourably with the good horses I've ridden in the past. His main asset is that he loves to race, that is very obvious when you ride him. And he has a very good turn of foot. For me, his best run of the year was at York in the Juddmonte. It was a strong field and he won very well.' Indeed, it is arguable that Rodrigo de Triano was the best 8-10 furlong horse Piggott had ridden since the days of Sir Ivor and Nijinsky; certainly Rodrigo was the best horse – he shared a Timeform rating of 130 with Royal Academy – Piggott partnered during the Second Coming.

There was one more pot of gold to chase: the Breeders' Cup in the sweltering sub-tropical heat and humidity of Florida's Gulfstream Park on October 31st. Chapple-Hyam and Piggott favoured the Mile on the grass but they were overruled by Sangster, who favoured the ten furlongs of the Classic on the dirt. 'Peter said he had had his way all season and so now I could make the decision. I feel Rodrigo has proved himself champion of Europe and if he were to win the Classic he would justifiably be world champion.'

Alas, Rodrigo de Triano finished stone-cold last. As he and Walter Swinburn struggled round the right Gulfstream circuit eating everyone's dirt, his regular partner was being ferried to hospital after an horrendous fall with Mr Brooks in the Sprint. Mr Brooks died. From her seat in the stand, Tracy Piggott screamed: 'Daddy's dead! Daddy's dead!' To many seated around her it seemed that she might be correct.

6

FLIRTING WITH DEATH

Like all jockeys Piggott was no stranger to falls and injuries. *The Sun* actually printed an annotated photo of Lester pointing out all his injuries for the enlightenment of its readers – punctured lung, broken leg, broken collar bone et al – in the wake of the Mr Brooks tragedy. A broken collar bone at Lincoln in March 1951 at the age of 15 started him off; two accidents stood out, however, due to the stark manner in which they unfolded before our eyes. In 1977 Lester freely admitted 'I'm lucky to be alive' after his Oaks mount Durtal bolted on the way to the start and her saddle slipped, trapping his foot in a twisted stirrup iron. The filly dragged him 100 yards and crashed through the rails; fortunately, they were plastic and the collision broke the iron. Two races later Piggott was back and on a winner. Then, in April 1981, also at Epsom, Piggott's right ear was almost torn off (31 stitches were required to repair the damage) as his horse Winsor Boy burst out from beneath the front of the stalls. Six days later, with his head swathed in so much bandage that it necessitated a larger helmet, Piggott returned, apparently none the worse; the following day he won the 1,000 Guineas on Fairy Footsteps. Lester Piggott was never short of 'bottle': 'The Iron Man of Racing', as one of his surgeons once called him. But this latest Florida escapade was viewed altogether differently. To the outside world Lester was now a frail, parchment-thin 56 – nearly 57–year-old grandfather whose fragility appeared endangered by contact with a strong breeze let alone dirt or turf at speeds in excess of 30 mph.

Nevertheless, if any one season of Piggott's Second Coming justified his return to the saddle it had to be 1992 for he rode the winners of 13 Pattern races. Riding good horses was the top and bottom of the comeback and thus, even more significantly, was the fact that eight of those 13 came in Group I events. In addition to Rodrigo de Triano's foursome, Piggott won the Gran Premio del Jockey Club e Coppa D'Oro at San Siro on Silvernesian for John Dunlop; the National Stakes at the Curragh on

Mr Brooks (far side) shows tremendous gameness to win Lester his tenth July Cup
(John Crofts)

O'Brien's Fatherland; and lastly, he rode the Richard Hannon-trained Mr Brooks to victory in the July Cup and the Prix de l'Abbaye.

Until the summer of 1992, Mr Brooks (a 5YO by Blazing Saddles named in honour of Mel Brooks who directed the spoof Western glorying in the same name as his sire) had spent his racing life in Ireland, whence he journeyed to Epsom for the 1990 Derby. Mr Brooks finished last and was put back to sprinting whereupon he landed a hat-trick of Irish Group IIIs during 1991. His first race for Richard Hannon was the 1992 King's Stand Stakes at Royal Ascot in which he and Piggott were only beaten half a length by Sheikh Albadou, winner of the Nunthorpe and Breeders' Cup Sprint in 1991, with Elbio, the King's Stand winner of 1991, a neck back in third. Fine performance though this was, there seemed no plausible reason for Mr Brooks to reverse the form with Sheikh Albadou in the July Cup over an extra furlong: indeed, Mr Brooks was only sixth best at 16–1 in a field of eight. The fierce gallop set by Shalford and Tbab insisted Piggott bide his time and he did not bring the white-faced Mr Brooks on to the scene until Sheikh Albadou had assumed control entering the final furlong.

'Mr Brooks has always been a good horse and he really showed it today. I was always on their heels and I knew he would pick them up when I asked him.' However, it was only by a rapidly diminishing head that Mr Brooks withstood a late flourish from Pursuit of Love, who had enjoyed anything but a trouble free passage on the inside. This was Piggott's tenth success in the July Cup and he was in a positively impish mood during the celebratory interview with Brough Scott, thrusting the purple cap he was due to wear in the next race over the interviewer's face in response to the inevitable question: 'How long can you go on?'

Mr Brooks then won a Group III in Berlin before going on to contest Europe's three remaining Group I sprints: the Nunthorpe; Haydock Park's Sprint Cup; and the Abbaye. At a difference of 26lb which more than favoured the 2YO sensation Lyric Fantasy he found the filly half a length too good for him at York, while at Haydock Sheikh Albadou won their 1992 rubber match by a cosy two-and-a-half lengths; but neither conqueror went to Longchamp and Mr Brooks was a slight odds on favourite for the Abbaye. He did not disappoint. 'Piggott is Mr Irresistible', is how *The Sporting Life* interpreted Mr Brooks's two length victory over Keen Hunter; 'Lester has still got the Abbaye habit', was the cringe-inducing equivalent in the *Post*. Next stop Gulfstream Park.

The European challenge for Breeders' Cup IX was considered the strongest ever mounted, including as it did the winners of the English and Irish 2,000 Guineas (Rodrigo de Triano), the Irish 1,000 Guineas (Marling), the Derby (Dr Devious) and the Prix de l'Arc de Triomphe (Subotica) plus previous Breeders' Cup winners in Sheikh Albadou and Arazi. The *Racing Post* devoted its entire front page to saying so in large bold type: in spite of Florida's excruciating 90 degree fahrenheit temperatures, debilitating 95 per cent humidity and the tight, intimidating character of the Gulfstream circuit, barely seven furlongs round and incorporating a pair of 180 degree bends.

As it happened, the Europeans were fortunate to deliver their challenge. On the ten-hour flight from London Stansted to Fort Lauderdale, the DC8 transport aircraft carrying Mr Brooks, Rodrigo de Triano and 16 other European horses plunged 500 feet in a matter of seconds upon striking a hot air pocket; the crates holding the horses were literally thrown around like matchboxes. Both Piggott's intended partners emerged from this ordeal miraculously unscathed. On arrival at Gulfstream, Mr Brooks was soon eating everything put in front of him and Rodrigo – recently sold for $6.2 million to stand at stud in Japan – staggered trackside clockers by covering three furlongs in 35 seconds in a dawn workout. Piggott arrived too late in the day for that particular gallop but he was exceptionally opti-mistic, by his standards, after partnering the colt on Friday morning. 'If

Rodrigo handles the dirt – and I was pleased to see the track was light and not deep and holding – he will win. He is the best miler in the world but the extra two furlongs will not present any problems.'

However, before Piggott went in search of the £975,000 first prize in the Classic there was Mr Brooks's attack on the Sprint to negotiate, whereby – five days short of his 57th birthday – he would become the oldest jockey to compete in the Breeders' Cup series, beating Bill Shoemaker by eight months. Shortly before 6.55pm GMT the 14 runners assembled at the six furlong gate located at the far end of the track. Sheikh Albadou and Walter Swinburn halted alongside Mr Brooks. 'Lester felt his horse moved terribly going to post', Swinburn related 20 minutes later. 'He doesn't usually say much so when he says something, you listen.'

The filly Meafara catapulted out of the gate in typically American style to initiate a pace as scorching as the temperature, which quickly relegated Mr Brooks to one of the tail-enders. Running the bend it became obvious that Piggott was concerned about something. He looked back, as if to check whether there was a horse immediately behind him. A split second later Mr Brooks's off-fore snapped. The horse began to pitch forward but Piggott, demonstrating the strength, balance and finesse of a rodeo rider, somehow kept the tottering animal upright long enough for the only horse behind them to get past and the imminent impact with the ground to be minimised. With a little bit more luck Piggott might have escaped scot-free but as the helpless jockey was hurled forward into the dirt his stricken partner rolled over and on to him. Pinned by half a ton of horse Piggott's body lay still. Paramedics rushed to the scene. While poor Mr Brooks writhed nearby, awaiting the lethal injection that would end his suffering, an oxygen mask was instantly clamped over Lester's face, a neck brace fitted, leg splints applied and a stretcher slipped underneath his unconscious form. All this was being observed in horrifying close-up on the closed-circuit television screens throughout the grandstands courtesy of a mobile cameraman. The ambulance sped away.

Tracy Piggott's fears that her father was fatally injured were thankfully unfounded. Word from the jockey's room was that Lester had been seen by Michael Roberts; he was conscious and sitting up; a cut head, broken collar bone and, perhaps, broken ribs were the only injuries. 'When the closed-circuit TV cameras zoomed in I saw he was still trapped under the horse and appeared to be unconscious', said Tracy Piggott. 'It was a hell of a shock. Within five minutes the doctors had an accurate picture of his injuries and I accompanied him in the ambulance to the hospital. Daddy looked an absolute fright with blood all over his face and dirt from the

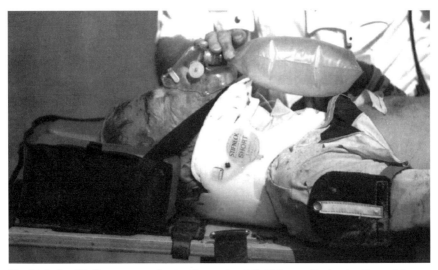

'Daddy's dead!': there were plenty of people at Gulfstream Park who thought Tracy Piggott might be proved correct *(AP,* Racing Post*)*

track. He looked so bad all sorts of things went through my mind. But an hour and a half later he was able to talk. All he wanted to know was who had won the race!'

Piggott was rushed to Hollywood Memorial Hospital in Hallandale where doctors diagnosed a broken left collar bone, two broken ribs and severe internal bruising: initial fear of a damaged spleen proved unfounded, although he had had a partially collapsed lung when first admitted; a brain scan was merely precautionary. The speed of Piggott's recovery astonished the Miami medical profession who reckoned he was 'the toughest sonofabitch racing has ever seen.'

Lester was soon sitting up eating jelly and ice cream – and speaking to reporters. J A McGrath of the *Daily Telegraph* was given the task of grilling the wounded jockey on behalf of the British press corps. Refused admission to the intensive care unit, he had to be content with calling Piggott's mobile from a pay phone in the hospital corridor.

Piggott's reply was characteristically unstated: 'I feel all right. I'm a bit stiff in the upper part of my body but that's only to be expected. I could ride again in three weeks if I wanted to; but the fact is that there is not much left as far as horses and races are concerned, so I'll probably take a rest. 'It's only a collar bone and a rib – I've had much worse falls tumbling out of bed! If it happened at Chepstow nobody would have given it a second thought. I will be riding again in Hong Kong in February. I knew Mr Brooks was going 20 yards before it happened. I looked behind on my left side to see what was following me. I did not want to stop suddenly with horses immediately behind. I remember him going down but I don't remember much after that. I must have been dazed. It's most unfortunate that it was a horse of Mr Brooks's ability. He was a lovely animal and would have won a lot of races next year.'

In addition to the call from McGrath, Piggott received a fax from the Queen wishing him well – not to mention an attempted visit from a tabloid reporter disguised as a doctor! Accordingly, a 17 stone security guard was posted outside his door and Piggott's name was removed from the hospital's computer. Piggott was released in time to celebrate his 57th birthday with a meal of lobster and chocolate cake. The *Sunday Mirror* got the pictures – Lester still nursing a big red bruise under his left eye – and the story. 'I can put up with pain. I'd rather die in bed than on a racetrack covered in dirt but we all have to go sometime....it's a frightening thing to be paralysed but none of the top jockeys think about it the way ordinary people do...nothing bothers me, they're going to stuff me when I go!'

After recuperating in the Florida sunshine for the best part of a fortnight Piggott jetted back into England on Sunday November 15th to find the Breeders' Cup, and particularly his accident, still the main topic of conversation in the racing community. The much-lauded European contingent had sunk almost without trace: two third places was the height of its achievement. 'If this race had been in England, I would have withdrawn Rodrigo', said Chapple-Hyam of his mud-caked fallen idol. 'Lester's the only one who knows him.'

Piggott's pre-race comments concerning Mr Brooks's action going to post had also attracted considerable attention. Why did he not withdraw Mr Brooks or at least inform the track vet of the problem? The horse often moved sluggishly before a race, countered Piggott and, perhaps he was stiff from the flight. When asked for their reaction to the incident, the American jockeys did not mince words. President of the American Jockeys Guild, Jerry Bailey, said: 'It's a judgement call and it's his butt. But in the same breath you might also take someone else with you, so you should have consideration of other riders and their horses.' Pat Day was even harsher: 'If the horse was really "off", then shame on him.' Richard Hannon, on the other hand, sprang to Piggott's defence: 'The horse was 100 per cent when he arrived in America and was 100 per cent right up to the start of the race. There was no way he would have been allowed to run if something was wrong. That sort of injury is a one-off. It could happen any time. Everyone saw that the horse was galloping well until there was a clean break of the leg. It's difficult to understand why he might have been moving badly going to the start – perhaps it was the dirt or maybe it was because the heat was so intense. But he had worked perfectly on that same bend for Lester the previous day and was in terrific form.'

The main story, naturally, concerned the possibility of Piggott's accident bringing about his retirement. 'Of course I'll be back. It's nonsense to say I will not ride again. I've got nothing else to do!' was Piggott's stock reply to all enquiries; but this could not prevent the press from canvassing opinion elsewhere.

Susan Piggott: 'There are some really gloomy articles in the newspapers talking about retirement but I don't believe Lester will be thinking that way. I believe his fitness will be a great contributory factor towards a speedy recovery. I don't think we have heard the last of him by any means.'

Maureen Piggott: 'He's enjoying himself and he's riding well. Why should he stop? Two weeks ago everyone was saying what a wonderful race he had ridden on Rodrigo de Triano to win the Champion Stakes – but now they are telling him to pack up.'

Robert Sangster: 'Carry on Lester! – that's what I say. I think he should carry on riding as long as he wants to. He can keep on riding for me as long as he likes. You will never tell Lester when he should stop.'

Geoff Wragg: 'Who are we to tell LP what to do? He's something on his own and only he will decide. Mentally it won't bother him, I'm sure. But at his age, physically it will knock him up.'

John Gosden: 'They never made any rules about Lester Piggott and we'd better not start now. He is his own man and does his own thing and I'm sure that's how it will continue.'

David Loder: 'Should hens be allowed to lay eggs?'

Willie Carson: 'Lester wouldn't want to quit on such a low note. He'll be back. Jockeys know the risks involved every time they get on a horse and Lester will have a better idea than most. It was an accident. It wasn't nice but he'll come through it.'

Claude Duval (The Sun): 'Please go...and go now! That's my passionate plea to Lester Piggott.'

PIGGOTT'S

Moment of disaster . . . a video shot shows Lester somersaulting between his horse and the Goodwood track as his protective cap goes flying

MIRACLE FALL

Amazing escape after terrifying spill shocks fans

RACING legend Lester Piggott had an amazing escape yesterday when he spectacularly crashed from his horse at 35mph.

by EDDIE FITZMAURICE

First the 58-year-old grandad – dubbed "superman" by his family – landed smack on his head.

Then, as his protective helmet flew

off, he bounced back up onto the air before coming down feet first.

Miraculously the heroes of the other galloping horses swerved surrounding Piggott by inches.

But horrified racegoers feared it was the end for the 11 times champion jockey as he lay motionless on the Goodwood track. Ambulancemen

who dashed to the rescue immediately put Piggott's neck in a brace and taped his head before stretchering him away.

But last night Lester – who has broken nearly every bone in his body during his glorious 46-year career – was laughing and joking in hospital.

Daughter Maureen Piggott said of a bang on the head, but he's

Turn to Back Page

Lester makes the front pages of the tabloids after a second horrendous spill in full view of the television cameras.

The *Racing Post* of November 2nd had promised: 'Great Survivor can triumph again in the face of adversity.' To no one's surprise he did. After holidaying in Singapore Piggott was champing at the bit for some action and found it in the hospitable environs of Dubai: the Nad Al Sheba racecourse on Friday, February 5th, 1993, was the appointed time and place for racing's own version of Lazarus to rise again. 'He'd been playing a lot of badminton to keep fit but I don't know how that could have worked', explained Tracy Piggott, 'because he manages to be able to stand there and move his arms and the other person is running all over the place. He doesn't seem to move!' Piggott had also indulged in plenty of swimming and walking and once in Dubai rode work every morning for trainer Dhruba Selvaratnam. 'If I had had a three-month lay-off I would have been blowing like a train after that', he said on dismounting from his first

7am workout. 'There was not so much as a puff. I like it here. This is as good a place as any to start after the accident. I am still not fully fit but I'm shaping well. The thought of retirement has never cropped up. I feel well and raceriding is all I know. I'd like to win the Derby once more before I retire to make it a nice figure of ten times.'

Lester had more time to gather his strength than he anticipated because a torrential storm flooded the Nad Al Sheba track, postponing the meeting from Friday to Sunday and, eventually, to the following Wednesday. All four Maktoum brothers were among the capacity 5,000 crowd to see Piggott finish a close second on two of his four mounts. He looked sure to celebrate his return with a winner on Sheikh Ahmed's Red Rainbow in the Jumairah Stakes until Shati and Richard Hills regained the lead to deny him by a head. Then, in the Zabeel Handicap, he put Greendale in front with a furlong to go only to be touched off by the fast finishing Polar Wind. Twenty four hours later the action switched to the Jebel Ali circuit, some 25 miles away, where the crowd rose to him as he kicked Bonita six lengths clear in the opening race; he followed up with a typically masterful frontrunning performance on Aghaadir. 'Not bad was it?' was the initial reaction. 'It has been a long time. I have missed riding and to win two felt good.' And a third winner – Raheena – followed the next day before Piggott set off for a month in Hong Kong prior to the onset of the British Flat season.

On Thursday July 28th, 1994, however, the 'should he or shouldn't he retire' debate resurfaced when Piggott took another crucifying fall in full view of the television cameras. Ironically, the horse involved, Coffee 'N Cream, was again one of Richard Hannon's: 'If I'm not careful Lester will be telling me I tried to kill him off twice!' Although the incident itself did not parallel that of Mr Brooks – the saddle slipped on this occasion – the resultant furore followed exactly the same pattern, albeit with even greater media hysteria since the accident occurred at home. The tabloid front pages whipped themselves into a frenzy. 'Lucky Lester' (*Daily Mirror* and *Daily Mail*); 'Lester Fall Horror' (*Daily Star*); 'Lucky 13; Bruised Lester escapes yet again in racing disaster number 13' (*The Sun*); 'Piggott's Miracle Fall' (*Today*). Even the editorials found space for some unwanted advice. 'He's a tough old nut...but isn't it time he enjoyed his sport like most other 58 year-olds: from the safety of an armchair in front of the telly?' (*Daily Star*); 'Hang up your whip, Lester. You've earned a rest.' (*The Sun*). *The Sun*, true to character, conducted one of its infamous telephone polls on the subject of whether he should finally call it a day. Lester's response to this tabloid hot air was terse in the extreme: 'There's been a lot of ******* rubbish written by you', he was quoted in the *Daily Express*. 'You're a load of *****. Just what is all the fuss about?'

What could not be denied was the ugly nature of Piggott's fall from Coffee 'N Cream. As the stalls opened for Goodwood's Ralph Hubbard Memorial Nursery the horse probably took a deep breath and jumped through its girths. Riding a horse with its saddle gradually slipping back over its quarters in a five furlong sprint down Goodwood's hill with firm ground threatening to greet you at any moment is not a set of circumstances to inspire confidence. Piggott spotted the problem straight away; twice he looked down at the girth. Yet he not only tried to ride a race he actually tried to launch a challenge in order to win it. It was at this point, a furlong out, with Coffee 'N Cream in second place, that the saddle finally gave way. As ever demonstrating the presence of mind born of more years raceriding than some already considered unwise, Piggott swung his right leg out of the stirrup but any hopes entertained of getting up on to the horse's withers and riding Coffee 'N Cream to a sensational victory were instantly dashed as all the gelding's tack came apart. Piggott conceded defeat and purposely slid feet first to the ground down the animals' left flank. The ensuing seconds bequeathed terrifying images. Piggott bounced sickeningly high – three to four feet – off the rock-hard turf, like a barrel off a runaway dray, his helmet being dislodged in the process. Even then, when most minds could be forgiven for going totally blank, Piggott's brain automatically coiled his body into the foetal position, with hands clasped behind the head for protection. Fortunately, the field numbered only half a dozen and by the time he finally hit the deck the others had been able to give him a wide berth.

Medics rushed to Piggott's aid in a dramatic reprise of Gulfstream Park; oxygen was administered, a neck brace fitted and his feet taped together before he was loaded into an ambulance bound for St Richard's Hospital, ten miles away in Chichester. Subsequent X-rays revealed nothing worse than severe bruising and three hours later Piggott promptly discharged himself. However, Michael Turner, the Jockey Club's chief medical advisor, was one doctor Piggott could not ignore: he stood Lester down for seven days, the statutory period for concussion. 'He told me he was keen to ride in Cologne on Sunday but I'm afraid he can't. Lester is quite bony and wouldn't bounce much so I think it must have been his body protector that helped him to bounce.'

The Piggott ladies were of one accord. Susan Piggott: 'Lester is absolutely fine and could ride tomorrow. In fact, he wants to! There are reddish marks on his face, presumably from grass burns, that's all. The fall looked horrendous with Lester bouncing so high. But it says a lot for the body protectors jockeys wear. He's as strong and as fit as he's ever been. What he may lack in youth he makes up for with experience, determination and judgement. Lester will know when the day is right for him to retire but it isn't now.'

Maureen Piggott informed *The Sun*: 'Quit? My daddy's Superman – he doesn't quit. A 58 year-old Lester Piggott does not compare to other 58 year-old men. Retirement is not a subject which has come up for discussion. He's fitter than most people 30 years younger. I don't think his age has anything to do with it. Having a fall is all part of racing. He could have been 19 and still fallen off. It did look like it was a very bad fall. He bounced a bit and was a bit lucky just to get off with concussion. Daddy's really annoyed because he will have to lay off racing for a week. He's itching to get back. Let's just say he's not pleased!'

Nor was Piggott best pleased by the acres of newsprint devoted to deciding his future. Channel 4's resident tribune of the people, John McCririck, was never one to prevaricate if asked for an opinion: 'Everyone in racing is conscious that if he has a really serious fall it will hang over us all forever. He's got to face up to it, that one day he must retire, whether it's at 60 or 70 years old. His reflexes cannot be the same as a young man's. How much longer can he go on? Everybody in racing is holding his breath when Piggott incidents like this happen. We all now live in daily dread that one day he will be carried off on a stretcher and will get such a severe injury due to his old bones that he will not be able to ride. How much better if he was to quit now while we can still remember the good days.' Nor did Willie Carson stand on ceremony. The *Daily Mirror* quoted him thus: 'I don't know why he keeps doing it but he is a law unto himself. If he keeps having falls like this the rest of us will not be able to afford the insurance. But he's tough as old boots. He's unique and we're all expecting him back in a couple of days. He wouldn't be Lester otherwise.'

The *Racing Post* pulled all the arguments together in a two-page spread entitled 'Lester and the future: Should he retire?' with John McCririck's 'Why it's time to go' countered by Paul Haigh's 'It's not time for the credits to roll.' Judged by the disposition of the resulting postbag, McCririck was in the minority; 'Sanctimonious Hogwash' being one of the more polite terms used to describe his view. Michael Turner had the last word, and he would always have the last word, so his contribution warranted respect: 'There are a lot of people who say Lester should do this and Lester should do that. When it has been determined whether or not he is fit to ride – and it will be for me to determine whether Lester is fit to ride in races –

then these people should discuss with him whether he considers it wise to reconsider.'

Down the years Lester Piggott had made 'cocking a deaf 'un' into something of an art form whenever unwelcome advice was in the air. 'Those people make me sick' he told *The Mail on Sunday*. 'What do they know about me, how I feel, how fit I am? I'll know when the day is right. No one else will tell me.'

In less than a week Piggott was back out on the gallops riding work and nine days after the accident he resumed raceriding with four mounts at Newmarket's televised meeting of August 6th. However, his very return epitomised the crossroads his career had now reached. Friday had been the intended day for his resumption but unable to secure any decent rides he chose to wait 24 hours for something more worthwhile. Good rides, the only rides Piggott was interested in, were becoming hard to find. All the big stables and big owners employed retained jockeys; the 'big owners' also meant the Maktoum family. Gone were the days when Lester could get a ride – or pinch a ride – merely by ringing the owner. Getting through to the Sheikhs could take all day; the Maktoum organisation had more chiefs than indians. Trainers, too, were becoming circumspect. 'I don't like putting him on horses with very little chance', said Ben Hanbury, for whom he was to ride En Attendant on the Saturday. 'But I am only too pleased to put him on a horse with a good chance because he is as good as anyone.' Dick Hern, no stranger to adversity himself and likewise never one to surrender to it, was putting Lester up on Tovarich: 'Lester is still equally as effective as he's ever been. His courage is still undaunted after all the knocks and ravages of time. The enthusiasm is there and he possesses a very good brain.'

Sadly, both En Attendant and Tovarich ran badly. Piggott's best ride proved to be The Jotter in the Sweet Solera Stakes for 2YO fillies; but having taken the lead the pair were caught on the post by Jural. This was a race, some said, Lester could have won and should have won. In a letter to *The Sporting Life*, journalist Noel Winstanley wrote: 'Here was an example of Lester trying to win cosily, looking across at his rivals when he should have been in the drive position, and, I might add, a performance of which in his prime he would not have been proud.'

Throughout the afternoon Piggott steadfastly refused all requests for an interview, including one from Channel 4. The idyllic Indian summer in which Lester had basked like a grinning cat was ending. The cheery Galloping Grandfather had gone. Old Stoneface was back. The walls had not only been re-erected, they were closing in.

7

GLOBETROTTING

Scarcely a corner of the world was left unexplored by Lester Piggott during his Second Coming. From Austria to Australia, from Buenos Aries to Bombay, Lester's travelling circus pitched its tent. He rode in two dozen countries, the majority of which were old haunts, such as the USA (first visited in 1955), Australia and India (both 1957), but several broke fresh ground. Up to 1985 he had won races in 26 different countries besides Britain; six more – Austria, Chile, Dubai, Macau, Slovakia and Turkey – would be added to the list between 1990 and 1995. Only Africa somehow escaped a visit, surprisingly so in view of his frequent appearances in South Africa from 1958 onwards and the links established in the republic through his cousin Fred Rickaby, once the country's most successful trainer. However, Lester's winter jaunt in the Far East, full of sunshine, old friends and wonderfully receptive crowds (plus, no doubt, equally wonderful appearance fees on occasions) continued to be an enjoyable method of both controlling his weight and obtaining a welcome respite from the vagaries of the English climate and the English media.

The rigours of globetrotting on this scale – even in first class – and the hazards of constant air travel are obvious to anyone who has stepped on to an aeroplane. Indeed, the dangers of flying so often were brought home to Piggott by an incident in English air space during August 1992. The twin-engined Piper Seneca aircraft in which he was flying from Newmarket to York with fellow jockeys George Duffield, Michael Hills and Philip Robinson on August 19th was suddenly approached by six jet fighters 4500 feet above RAF Waddington, near Lincoln. As the Tornados tore past one got to within a few feet – Robinson swore he saw the whites of the pilot's eyes – of the Piper. Piggott was reading a newspaper at the time: 'We went into the slipstream of the jet and the plane dropped very quickly and we hit the roof. It was frightening and we were very lucky. We were nearly blown away.' The snoozing Duffield awoke with a start to find

Lester's head in his lap and pilot David Smith calling "Mayday! Mayday!" into his radio. Smith, a former RAF pilot himself, made an emergency landing at Waddington in order to have his plane checked for any damage (the down draught from the Tornado had flipped the Piper on to its back) before continuing the flight. Fortunately, the jockeys had been belted-in and suffered nothing more than superficial head and neck injuries. An official enquiry, which criticised Waddington's air traffic controllers, came to the conclusion that the planes came within ten feet of a collision.

Wherever Lester roamed during the Second Coming, victory was accompanied by the customary Piggott baggage of fines, bans and bust-ups. The trend was set even before he stepped on to foreign soil when the French authorities appeared reluctant to issue him with a licence. Article 47 paragraph two of the French Rules of Racing – a new ruling introduced in 1989 – stated: 'To be allowed to ride as a jockey it is necessary to have an age of over 18 but less than 50'. French racing supremo Louis Romanet was quick to confirm: 'Unfortunately, we cannot make an exception for Piggott'. However, not for the first time, racing *did* make an exception for Lester Keith Piggott.

Within 48 hours, a special meeting of the stewards of the Societe d'Encouragement – the French equivalent of the Jockey Club – had convened to discuss the matter and a spokesman immediately announced: 'On advice of our lawyers the stewards have decided that Piggott must see a doctor of our choice before being allowed back in the saddle. This decision has been made because he is over 45 years of age and we consider this case a special one. Every aspect of Piggott's health will be gone into in great detail.'

Piggott's date with the doctors was arranged for October 30th; he cancelled it and rode at Redcar instead. The following day he did consent to cross the Channel – foregoing two rides at Yarmouth – and underwent a series of tests at Maisons-Laffitte. Piggott had the offer of two decent mounts at Saint-Cloud on the Sunday and was keen to get cracking. The plan struck another hitch. The doctor who examined him had requested details of earlier blood and heart tests to be sent to the Societe's offices but when the fax arrived on November 1st they were unattended owing to a public holiday.

'I took the trouble to go over there and undergo a medical exactly to avoid problems but they're messing me about', Piggott complained. 'I have to send another load of papers about tests I have already taken here. Let's hope they don't want something else. It's not much of an example of Common Market co-operation. The Irish and Americans accepted my fitness to ride on production of an English medical certificate but the French insist on doing their own.'

After a week littered with red tape, the saga was eventually resolved on the Friday and Piggott duly rode at Saint-Cloud – fruitlessly as it turned out. The breakthrough French winner was not far off, however; arriving on November 17th, down in the provinces thanks to Bashful Boy, trained by William Hastings-Bass, who won the Prix Maurice-Edouard Delanglade at Parc Borely in Marseilles. Piggott finally scored on the main metropolitan tracks at the end of the month as Dear Doctor landed the Prix le Fabuleux at Maisons-Laffitte. He rounded off the year in true Piggott style: he picked up a four-day ban at Saint-Cloud on December 4th for being adjudged to have made insufficient effort on Lady Isis in the Prix Cherie Noire.

Lady Isis (a daughter of Durtal, the filly who almost killed Piggott before the start of the 1977 Oaks) redressed the balance by providing Piggott with an armchair victory at Maisons-Laffitte the following March but Lester's affairs with French fillies in 1991 were not always so rewarding. In the Poule d'Essai des Pouliches – the French 1,000 Guineas – he partnered Caerlina and the pair were nearly brought down in an accident with La Carene shortly after the start which relegated them to last place. In the straight Caerlina responded gamely to Piggott's driving to finish a rapidly-closing third to the odds-on favourite Danseuse du Soir. 'With better luck we'd have been second but I don't think we'd have won', was all the jockey would say about a rough race which saw La Carene's rider Eric Legrix suspended for four days. Caerlina's chance in the French Oaks – the Prix de Diane – was self-evident and her victory not unexpected but Piggott was not in the saddle. For once, it was he who had been jocked-off and, of all people, the beneficiary was Eric Legrix. Caerlina belonged to Kaichi Nitta, a highly superstitious Japanese owner, who insisted on a change of jockey in view of the bad luck encountered in the Pouliches.

Apart from Mr Brooks's Prix de l'Abbaye success of 1992, the highspot of Piggott's Gallic sorties came in 1993. At the prestigious Deauville fixture, Chapel Cottage took the Group II Prix Maurice de Gheest and Danse Royale the Group III Prix de Pysche, while in Longchamp's Prix du Pin (Listed) he partnered the Queen's Sharp Prod to a brilliant victory, dictating the pace throughout the seven furlongs but keeping enough in reserve to hold the late thrust of Acteur Francais by a length.

Sharp Prod and Piggott were soon reunited for the Grosser Silicon Bavaria Sprint-Preis in Munich, which they won by a neck – though Piggott was fined £60 by the stewards for excessive use of the whip. This

Chapel Cottage lands the Prix Maurice de Gheest at Deauville (John Crofts)

was the partnership's second German success as it had landed the previous year's Group II Moet & Chandon-Rennen at Baden-Baden.

Piggott had been plundering German prizes almost as long as he had been stealing those of the French: he won the first of three German Derbies (on Orsini) back in 1958 three years after his initial French success on Patras in Longchamp's Prix St Roman. His first ever ride in Germany was at Dusseldorf, also in 1955, so it was fitting that he should make his return to Germany at the same track on November 21st, 1990. Bolstered by a strong presence from the British Army on the Rhine, the crowd of 8500 saw him finish second on Lianka in the opening race but unplaced on his other three mounts, all four well-backed odds-on favourites.

An even greater throng – pushing 36,000 – packed Berlin's revamped Hoppegarten on April 14th, 1991, to watch Piggott take part in the first meeting at the course since German reunification. Sponsored by Holsten Breweries, Piggott rode in four races without claiming any success (he returned to Hoppegarten in 1992 to win the Group III Grosser Preis von Berlin on Mr Brooks). The onset of summer, however, heralded a purple patch.

Sizzling Saga got the ball rolling by easily winning Munich's Grosser Tiffany Sprint-Preis but the momentum really picked up during the Baden-Baden meeting at the end of August. On Sunday the 25th Piggott rode a double for owner Willi Bechmann, on Tao in the Group III Furstenberg Rennen and Glen Flight in the Preis der Casino Baden-Baden (Listed); on the Wednesday he partnered his faithful Chepstow ally Nicholas to victory in the Group II Jacobs Goldene Peitsche, thus achieving the biggest success of his wife's four-year training career; and on the 30th he notched another double courtesy of Northern Hal in the Preis der Stadt Baden-Baden (Listed) and Showbrook in the Moet & Chandon Rennen (Group II) for Peter Walwyn and Richard Hannon respectively. On the second Sunday, Lester recorded his sixth victory of the week on Maitre to become the leading jockey at the meeting and earn himself a commemorative crystal vase.

Piggott's German prospects for 1992 seemed even rosier with the announcement that he had agreed to ride the horses of Arnold Nothdurft, a retired window manufacturer who had recently purchased 16 horses at an estimated cost of £1.5 million with a view to making his mark on the German racing scene. Nothdurft paid £280,000 for Germany's top 2YO of the previous season, the unbeaten Vicenzo, and at the Newmarket Autumn Sales of 1991 he bought the 3YO Friedland out of Henry Cecil's stable for 56,000 guineas. The latter got the association off to a flying start by winning the Express Grand Prix Aufgallop 92 (Listed) at Cologne on March 22nd but Vicenzo disappointed badly on his seasonal debut behind Platini in the Dr Busch Memorial at Krefeld in April – though Piggott did win the Gestut Olympis Spring Cup (Listed) on Canadian Prince. Thereafter the relationship between owner and jockey quickly turned sour. At the end of May, Friedland finished last in a valuable handicap and soon afterwards Nothdurft dispensed with Piggott's services, saying he was 'disappointed with Piggott's attitude'.

Lester was far from finished with Germany, however. In 1993 he again won the Preis der Stadt Baden-Baden, on this occasion aboard Lucky Guest for John Dunlop's stable, and in 1994 he made all on Tommy Stack's Oenothera to win the Robert Pfedmenges Rennen (Listed) at Hoppegarten. Then, at Baden-Baden in August, Lester went out with a bang, winning a handicap on the locally-trained Elegante and receiving a two-day suspension for causing interference on Zimzalabim in the day's big race.

Italy was another old stamping ground to yield rewarding trips throughout the Second Coming although, as in France, the first win came at one of the lesser venues rather than the major tracks of San Siro in Milan and the Capannelle in Rome: Ghilly Dhu, in the Premio Sedan, a five furlong handicap at Livorno on November 15th, 1990, being the animal to work the oracle. Lester quickly followed up with a brace at the Capannelle a fortnight later on Cocofrio and Bateau Rouge. Bigger fish were to be netted in Italian waters aboard raiders from Arundel. John Dunlop made a habit of pirating Italy's more weakly contested Pattern races and on October 27th, 1991 he gave Piggott the ride on Alhijaz in the Group I Gran Criterium for 2YOs at San Siro, a race he had won twice before. Piggott and Alhijaz comfortably brought off the hat-trick, making smooth progress out of the pack to beat another English colt, Governor's Imp, by two-and-a-half lengths.

Almost a year to the day Piggott and Dunlop teamed up again for a second Group I success at San Siro with Silvernesian in the Gran Premio del Jockey Club e Coppa d'Oro. Piggott jumped the 3YO son of Alleged out of the stalls and, as he had on the colt's father in the 1977 Arc, proceeded to lead his rivals a merry dance. Coming just 24 hours after Rodrigo de Triano's victory in the Champion Stakes, Silvernesian's win completed a momentous weekend for Piggott since it included the two richest European prizes he collected during his comeback; furthermore, it raised his total of Group I successes in 1991 to eight, a figure equalled at the time by only Pat Eddery (who later added a ninth).

Finally, in May 1994, Piggott inspired Dunlop's Captain Horatius to a nose win over Big Tobin in the Group II Premio Ellington at the Capannelle before doubling up in the Premio Lazio on the Luca Cumani-trained Suplizi. Some gloss was taken off the occasion as the stewards fined Piggott 500,000 lira (about £200) for failing to take the mount on Lazy Duke in a claiming race. The horse was set to carry only 8 stone 5lb, a weight Piggott had not made since 1979.

This was not the first time that Italian stewards had deprived Lester of some hard-earned lire. In March 1991, he was fined one million lire by the Pisa stewards despite passing the post first in the Premio Scuola Normale on Wild Grouse. The real villain of the piece was the horse's trainer Mario Gasparini who had forgotten to put the weight cloth under Piggott's saddle – which meant the winning jockey weighed-in three kilos light. Accordingly, Wild Grouse – a hot 5–2 favourite – was disqualified and Gasparini fined three million lire and reported to the Jockey Club Italiano. Wild Grouse did compensate Piggott with facile victories in the Premio Conte Demonio in Florence and the Premio Bereguardo (Listed) at San Siro, the latter on the same afternoon as Lester won the Premio Bimbi (Listed) on Jack Berry's Bit-A- Magic. Not that the Italian penalties ever ceased. In June 1992, Piggott drew a five-day suspension for causing interference in a race at the Capanelle; and in October 1993 the San Siro officials fined him five million lire for taking the wrong course and then pulling up his mount in the Premio Duca d'Aosta.

Europe's smaller fry did not elude Piggott's net: he rode in Denmark, Belgium, Sweden, Norway, Slovakia, Austria, Spain, Switzerland and Turkey.

Spain was the first stop on November 18th, 1990 (a second place from two rides at La Zarzuela in Madrid) but Sweden proved the most eventful destination. Things began sweetly enough. Thirty-three years after he won the Svenskt Derby on Flying Dutchman, Lester made a triumphant return to Malmo's Jagersro racecourse on August 11th, 1991, to win the race for a second time, riding the German-trained Tao. The combination prevailed by a record 13 lengths. A fortnight later, the duo added the Group II Furstenberg-Rennen at Baden-Baden. Tao was even rumoured to be a possible mount in the Prix de l'Arc de Triomphe until the colt's sudden death curtailed any such speculation.

The 1994 Svenskt Derby, by contrast, was memorable for all the wrong reasons. Piggott was due to partner Zerenad in the Derby plus five other horses on the afternoon of August 6th and the racecard not only bore his smiling face on the cover but also contained a full-page article about him. The only snag was that Piggott had agreed to ride the Queen's Sharp Prod at Hoppegarten on the same day. 'Racing is not a big sport here and this was the greatest day of our year', said Jagersro official Stefan Jansen. 'When Piggott rides it gets a lot of publicity because he is a name the Swedish press knows. We printed the racecards on August 1st. On August 2nd we got a fax from Piggott saying that due to his fall at Goodwood he would not be able to come. Then we found out he would be riding in Germany. We were not very pleased.' Jagersro, reported to have lost £15,000 in advertising revenue because of Piggott's non-appearance, could do nothing other than impose a 3,000 kroner fine – a paltry £250. Sharp Prod, some might say quite justly, got beaten!

But where Lester Piggott is concerned, racing authorities have short memories and before August was out Piggott was the star attraction for Sweden's first ever Group race, the Stockholm Cup at Taby, in which he was to partner Captain Horatius. 'It's great to have Lester here', said Taby spokesman Bo Gillborg. 'I'm sure the other matter is now fully forgiven.' Captain Horatius finished second; Piggott paid his fine. Clearly, mountainous countries beginning with the letter S did not agree with Lester: the Swiss only race once a week yet Lester still managed to receive a two-day suspension from them in May, 1991.

Central and Eastern Europe were much more hospitable, with Lester making initial visits to the winner's enclosure in Austria, Slovakia and

Quite like old times as the Queen's colt Sharp Prod is virtually lifted past the post in the Moet & Chandon-Rennen at Baden-Baden in September 1992 *(John Crofts)*

Turkey. John Dunlop provided the Turkish success on October 2nd, 1991, when Lucky Guest won the Group II Topkapi Trophy at Veliefendi. Twenty-five thousand packed the Istanbul track to see Lucky Guest defeat the French colt Past Master by two lengths. 'I had a perfect ride and was very impressed with the state of the track', said Piggott.

After winning the Internationale Standard Meile at Vienna's Freudenau in 1993 (one of a treble at the Austrian course), Piggott and Lucky Guest tried for a repeat Topkapi success in 1993 only to find one too good for them. However, Lucky Guest did not play a part in one of Piggott's most spectacular European exploits: the weekend before the 1993 Topkapi Trophy, Lester rode five winners in two different countries on the same day. On the afternoon of Sunday, July 18th, he won the Slovanske Derby in Bratislava on Zimzalabim (then trained by Barry Hills) and completed his hat-trick on Laten and Fiorentia before dashing 35 miles across the Austro-Slovakian border to notch an evening double at Freudenau on Akenside and, more importantly, Soft Call in the Preis der Diana, the Austrian Oaks. Winning a Derby and an Oaks in one day was a novel achievement, even in the record-breaking world of Lester Piggott.

In spite of these assorted meanderings around Europe nothing quite held a candle to the exotic annual winter tour of the Far East, invariably centred on a stint in Hong Kong. For the first comeback tour of 1991 everybody wanted a piece of the action. The show opened in India where Piggott had not ridden in 22 years. One of the country's leading owners, Vijay Mallya, engaged him for the Indian Derby, held at Bombay's Maha-lakshmi racetrack on February 3rd, an event sponsored by Mallya's UB Group, an international brewing and chemicals conglomerate. 'Because we are involved in the sponsorship we would like to make sure we get good publicity for the race. There is no better publicity than having Lester Piggott ride. I am bringing in Lester not only to ride for me but also so that the Indian racing public can see one of the all-time greats. I'm sure he's as good as ever; talent dies hard. I am sure he will put up a good show for us.'

The question on everyone's lips – as with any Derby – was 'What does Lester ride?', because Mallay owned six of the entries. After lengthy last-minute consultations between owner, trainer and jockey the choice fell on the filly Speedbird, impressive winner of her only race. In front of an estimated 100,000 racegoers – 'The atmosphere here is unbelievable. It is the richest race we have ever run but most of the excitement is being generated by the fact that we have Piggott here', explained the Royal Western India Turf Club – Speedbird was sent off the 5–1 second favourite but she proved a massive flop, finishing among the tail-enders. Lester, however, still did his stuff, winning on Scorpio, which was the most popular outcome on the ten-race card.

On to Hong Kong. Over 32,000 filed into Sha Tin on February 9th (4000 more than on a normal Saturday) only to gawp at the sight of Piggott riding five losers. 'I don't think three of them had much chance anyway and the other couple ran fair races. I've been getting around a bit over the last few days and I hope I can get on a couple more that have really good chances next Sunday at Happy Valley. It's a competitive place, Hong Kong, and you can't just walk in and expect to get on anything. But I've been told that there are good rides for me and I'm happy enough with that at the moment.' As it happened, Piggott failed to unearth one winner during the entire stay. He had come primarily to partner Tarnside Turbo for his old friend, and prominent local businessman, Tony S.K. Wong in the £135,000 Hong Kong Derby on February 24th. Unfortunately, the horse was balloted out; the only other chance of a ride rested with Mastermind, in the care of Patrick Biancone. 'He didn't run well in the Hong Kong Classic Trial,' said the dual Arc-winning French trainer, 'and I think this is a little too rich for him at the moment.'

At the eleventh hour Biancone changed his tune and decided to let Mas-termind take his place in the 14-runner line-up. 'I do not think a world-class jockey like Lester Piggott should be sitting in the stands when a race like this is being run in Hong Kong. I am also convinced that if Master-mind is to have a chance it will only be because Piggott is riding him.'

Mastermind was brought with a typical whirlwind flourish to snatch sixth spot behind the undefeated 7–2 favourite River Verdon, who eventually developed into the most popular horse in the Colony after a string of big-race victories. 'Mastermind didn't really stay the trip', reported Piggott. 'But we were going to make the frame, I thought, until we were squeezed out of it in the last 100 metres.' Then, once he had hosted a farewell lunch at the plush Regent Hotel for fellow jockeys John Matthias (who rode River Verdon), John Reid and Tony Ives, Piggott flew back to India where he steered Mallya's gelding Delage to an explosive last-to-first victory in the Indian Turf Invitation Cup at the Guindy racecourse in Madras.

Piggott's effect on the Mahalakshmi turnstiles guaranteed his return for the 1992 Indian Derby. 'When he rode in last year's race there was no chance of getting a ticket days before the meeting', said Mallya's co-owner Zavaray Poonawalla. 'It's the same this year and I do hope he wins it. They love him here.' After a brief stopover in Dubai where he rode four winners from five rides at a meeting for Arab horses, the RWITC's top drawcard arrived safely. Keeping him company in the gate for the 1992 Derby were Willie Carson and Frankie Dettori; his old Scottish adversary came out best on this occasion by finishing a short-head second to the favourite Astonish while Piggott (on Desert Mirage) and Dettori (Golden Horn) never got into contention. Lester did not leave Bombay winnerless; a superbly timed challenge got top weight Clark Gable up to win the Royal Hong Kong Jockey Club Trophy.

Although it took longer than anyone could have imagined Piggott eventually found his way into the Sha Tin winner's circle on February 20th, 1993, the successful conveyance being So Easy, trained by long-standing friend Ivan Allan, for whom he won the 1984 St Leger on Commanche Run. It was an eventful day. Piggott was unable to make the weight for one ride which prompted stewards to draw his attention to Hong Kong's rules of racing, while another mount – the aptly named Beat Them Up – was withdrawn after it had thrown its head back and clouted Piggott in the face, necessitating three stitches.

Two weeks later So Easy delivered the first leg of Piggott's first Hong Kong double in 18 years; the second leg at Sha Tin came from Dashing. Nevertheless, the Colony yielded few 'So Easy' opportunities in 1993 or 1994. In fact, matters dipped so alarmingly on the '94 trip – two winners in six weeks – that Piggott cut short his stay. Not, however, before he became the first jockey to ride in Hong Kong and Macau on the same day.

Upon completing his final stint at Sha Tin on March 27th he caught the ferry to Macau for seven rides at the Taipa track. Surplus never got into the hunt in the Macau Derby but he did not come away empty-handed since Real Best secured one of the supporting events.

What proved to be Piggott's farewell tour was fittingly the grandest of all, straddling three continents and four months. It commenced in December 1994 in Chile and concluded in the United Arab Emirates in April 1995 by way of India, Singapore and Australia. From Chile (one winner) Lester travelled over the Andes to Argentina for the Grade I Gran Premio Copa de Plata Arquitecto Roberto Vasquez Mansilla at San Isidro which commemorated the man who restored the Buenos Aries course to its former glory after it had been closed for several years by the 'generals' in the 1970s. Piggott finished ninth of the 21 runners on Southern Bell, having suffered considerable interference.

Piggott enjoyed better luck at a second celebratory event in January, a Bombay fixture in honour of the 24th Asian Racing Conference: he rode Nora to victory in the McDowell Multi Million. Then it was on to Australia, which – as in 1986 – was intended to be the final port of call: the difference, and a crucial difference, being that in 1995 there had been no announcement of impending retirement or any indication this was turning into a global lap of honour. Nevertheless, he had no sooner touched down in Sydney than heavy hints were being cast in that direction.

The frank admission of a new-found *laissez faire* attitude to his sport which surfaced during an interview with John Tapp on Sky TV's *Inside Running* programme contrasted starkly with traditional Piggott philosophy: 'I don't take my raceriding too seriously these days. I accept that I'm not going to get offered as many rides because of my age and my opportunities are drying up. But that is a situation which suits me, I can coast along and enjoy my riding. It's easy riding just a few times a week. I can't go on forever. It's life though, isn't it? It happens to everybody. You can't stay young forever and that's the way it is.'

Piggott's Australian visit was meant to be a brief respite from commitments in Singapore and any raceriding nothing more than a busman's holiday while he stayed with Kulnara-based, but Irish-born, trainer Kevin Connolly, the provider of his solitary Macau winner in 1994. 'Lester was a hero of mine when I was young and he rode many winners for my father Michael in Ireland and England during the 60s and 70s', said Connolly. 'Lester has done it all in racing and it is a real honour to have him ride one for me at Rosehill. It would be great if we won but it would be a bit bullish of me if I said Zadok will beat Strategic who is obviously very good.'

Zadok indeed failed to lower Strategic's colours but Connolly's 2YO ran so invitingly for Piggott that the flying visit scheduled to last two weeks actually stretched – on and off – to two months and developed into a mini-tour of its own. Besides the major metropolitan tracks in Sydney, Melbourne and Canberra, Lester sampled the more rustic delights of Quirindi, Albury, Wellington, Caloundra, Toowoomba and Fannie Bay in much the same way as he had patronised the country tracks of Ireland: not so much a walkabout as a rideabout. If the expenses were agreeable Lester would travel. So successful was this extended Australian sojourn that his total of eight winners proved two more than he had achieved in 1986.

Piggott's appearance at Sydney's Rosehill on February 11th to ride Zadok in the Euclase Handicap and Air Seattle (for Clarrie Connors) in the Satellite Stakes was eagerly anticipated by the locals. 'Lester rides into sunset: last chance to see the legend in action', declared the *Daily Telegraph Mirror*. An extra 2,000 paying customers were attracted through the turnstiles and even though Lester won neither race he received, according to one scribe, 'a reception generally reserved for brilliant cricketer Shane Warne when he takes five wickets.'

All the jockeys were pleased to see him. 'In his prime Lester was probably the best jockey I've seen', said three-times Sydney champion Kevin Moses, while up-and-coming champion apprentice Corey Brown confessed to feeling a little nervous just being in the same jockeys' room: 'I hope to be able to introduce myself to Lester and have a chat with him. He has achieved so much in racing and just to meet the bloke is going to be a great thrill but to be actually riding in a race against him is unreal. At least I will always be able to say I rode against Lester Piggott.'

The Rosehill stewards also seemed pleased to see Lester – they duly requested the pleasure of his company at an enquiry into some scrimmaging which occurred in Zadok's race. Lester had taken Zadok across to the fence in order to lead at the first turn.' I knew there were at least two horses on my inside', he told the AJC chief steward John Schreck. 'My horse wanted to go forward but the rest didn't, so I pushed ahead.' Film evidence clearly showed Lester taking two or three long looks on his inside before allowing Zadok to cross and he was exonerated from blame.

Mr Schreck had not finished with him, however. He issued him with a warning for weighing-in half a kilo over and then denied him permission to accept an invitation from the committee of the Sydney Turf Club to join them during the afternoon: jockeys, insisted Schreck, were only permitted to do so after the last race.

'Piggott finds a real opal down under': Lester and Zadok after winning the GrII A $205,000 Black Opal Stakes in Canberra (Steve Hart/Pacemaker)

Controversy and Lester Piggott were, of course, bedfellows with more than a passing acquaintance: four days later they bumped into each other again after an incident-packed race at Warwick Farm in Sydney's south western suburbs. Piggott was once more hauled before the stewards on a charge of causing interference. In trying to get a clear run on Recollect in the Derma Wash Handicap he shifted in sharply toward the rail from his position in the centre of the track and in the process squeezed-up two opponents. Donning his wig and gown, Lester gave his powers of advocacy free rein and protested his innocence – and was let off with a severe reprimand! 'We don't accept that kind of riding from our jockeys', said acting chief steward Ian Paterson. 'Next time we will have to take some action.' However, the sparks began to fly when New Zealander Grant Cooksley, on the other hand, received a hefty suspension for interference he had caused in the same race, a decision which left the incensed Kiwi fuming sarcastically: 'It is a pity that I am not English and old otherwise I might have been luckier!'

The 'lucky old Englishman' was consequently at liberty to fulfil his engagements in Sydney and Canberra the following weekend, and right royally did he capitalise on his good fortune. 'Piggott pounces' was the *Sydney Telegraph*'s headline in response to his victory on So Keen in the A$40,000 Analie Plate at Randwick on February 18th.

Riding the Graeme Rogerson-trained mare with supreme confidence, he tracked pacemaker Miss Kariba for most of the six furlongs before making his move close home to win by a short neck. 'I can't get the rides I used to but I still enjoy riding a winner no matter where it is.' On the Sunday he rode two more in Canberra: Roll On By and, more significantly, Zadok in the A$50,000 Black Opal Preview. Piggott jumped the 7–4 favourite to the lead straight from the barrier and expertly controlled the tempo of the race. Restraining Zadok at a deceptive gallop, he did not finally give the gelding his head until well into the straight. Zadok responded in style, quickly bursting five to six lengths clear to clock a very fast time and book his place in the Black Opal proper, a Group II event worth A$205,000 over the same six furlongs on March 5th. 'Piggott finds a real opal down under', opined *The Australian*.

After a fruitless visit to Quirindi, in northern New South Wales, for the Quirindi Cup meeting on February 20th, Piggott's itinerary called for a return to Singapore, where he was hoping to bid for an unprecedented fourth Lion City Cup at Bukit Timah, having recorded a hat-trick between 1976 and 1978. However, the prospect of a fancied ride in a top race guaranteed he would pick up the threads of his busman's holiday in Australia, and he was immediately snapped up by leading trainer Lee Freedman for rides at Flemington's rich autumn carnival in Melbourne the weekend following the Black Opal.

The Toohey's-sponsored Black Opal proved a veritable tour-de-force. 'Piggott calls the shots in pillar-to-post win', wrote Jack Elliott of a vintage Piggott performance in a race which, just for once, really did replicate the exact pattern of its 'preview'. The 6–4 favourite led all the way as he had two weeks earlier, although on this occasion only having three-quarters of a length to spare over his closest pursuer, Ravarda, at the finish.

Lester's subsequent appearance at Flemington – principally to partner Our Pompeii in the A$600,000 Australian Cup – provoked a more mixed reaction. While scoring heavily in the popularity stakes, boosting the gate and being cheered to the echo every time he vacated the jockeys' room to ride or sign autographs, he drew a blank on the track and his riding even attracted some adverse comments from Melbourne journalists. One critic, plainly less charitable than his Sydney and Canberra counterparts, gleefully resorted to landing the lowest of low blows: 'He was once the greatest but he is anything but now!'

Piggott may have lost the Flemington round of his battle with Melbourne's killjoys but he was not about to leave the city without drawing blood; he put the doubters to shame with a lethal demonstration of quintessential 'Piggott Power' at Caulfield on March 19th. Swift Encounter was just a 20–1 longshot for the Woodcock Handicap. Somehow Piggott forced him to the front at the top of the straight but he was soon headed and entitled, as his odds warranted, to have hastily capitulated. Piggott was having none of it. Up went the right arm and Swift Encounter's rump felt the full force of its stinging wand as Piggott vigorously drove her back into contention magically to snatch the lead in the very last stride.

The remainder of Piggott's 1995 Australian 'rideabout' centred on the so-called 'bush meetings' up country. He had already journeyed over the Blue Mountains to Wellington, some 250 miles to the north west of Sydney, to participate on March 13th in the Race Club's Carlton Wellington Boot Carnival, an Irish-style festival featuring a variety of social events – golf, bowls, a Grand Ball – in addition to the racing. Lester helped himself to a winner, riding Toy Account. Then he notched a double on Lagisquet and Galway (a first win for trainer Tony Kelly, son-in-law of former Malton jockey Lionel Brown) at Albury on the New South Wales-Victoria border. The Race Club was delighted with a crowd 3,000 higher than usual, which, needless to say, plunged heavily on Lester's mounts. However, despite six rides at Caloundra (March 28th) and Toowoomba (March 30th), to the north and west of Brisbane respectively, he failed to add to the eight successes thus far accumulated; he began to eye the forthcoming prestigious Sydney Carnival where the premier races included Golden Slipper, AJC Derby and the Sydney Cup.

'My plans are at present uncertain', he told Jack Elliott. 'I'm waiting to see what is happening in Sydney at the Carnival. There are some good horses racing there and I hope to ride some of them in the big races. Everything at present is a little up in the air. I'm enjoying myself in Australia. It's a wonderful country and the people here have been very kind to me. It is my intention to come back again after the English season and I would like to have a ride in the Melbourne Cup. That has always been an ambition of mine.'

Piggott's hopes fell flat. While the AJC Derby was being run at a lush and palatial Randwick on April 15th he was experiencing two frustrating rides amid the swaying palm trees and T-shirted sunseekers at the Darwin Turf Club's Fannie Bay racecourse, up in the tropical Northern Territory, on a track composed of sand treated with sump oil. Australians have a notoriously ambivalent attitude toward sporting champions. Quick to elevate their heroes to pedestal status and quick to try and knock them off – or, to put it in the vernacular, 'Lop the tall poppy.' Lester was clearly still regarded as 'tall poppy', for while *The Sunday Territorian* wrote generously:

An Arabian night: an unlikely location for the final curtain *(Trevor Jones)*

'He still gave a good exhibition of his high-in-the-irons European style that has seen him win a string of Classics', *The Australian* headed its report with: 'Lester's light dims as Torchbearer plods in', and quoted one disgruntled – doubtless, financially embarrassed – Ocker as moaning, 'Jeez, what a shocker of a ride' after Lester's mount, the 3–1 favourite and tearaway early leader in the Jim Beam Handicap, faded ingloriously to cross the line sixth in a field of eight. Subsequently asked if he would like a special commemorative acknowledgement from the course commentator over the public address system at the end of the meeting Lester declined. He dragged the saddle from Torchbearer's back and walked quietly away. The surprisingly successful Australian adventure of 1995 was over.

Torchbearer, however, was not destined to enter pub-quiz lore as the final competitive conveyance of Lester Keith Piggott. On his way home to Britain Lester stopped off in the United Arab Emirates. Fourteen rides at Jebel Ali, Nad Al Sheba and Abu Dhabi unfortunately yielded no winners, merely two second places. The second of them came on his last appearance. The 5YO gelding Northern Bound was his partner in the Omeir Bin Youssef (Buick) Abu Dhabi Championship over one mile three furlongs at the Abu Dhabi Equestrian Club on Friday, April 28th; they were beaten six-and-a-half lengths by Karoo Lark ridden by Peter Brette, once an apprentice with Rae Guest in Newmarket, who thus goes down in history as the last man to beat Lester Piggott.

8

THE AMMUNITION
RUNS OUT

Some people were trying to retire Lester Piggott almost as soon as he climbed off Lupescu's back. A few more reckoned that the euphoric aftermath of Belmont Park provided the ideal opportunity; and, inevitably, the falls of Mr Brooks and Coffee 'N Cream swelled the chorus of 'Lester, please retire' to Wagnerian proportions. Lester continued to 'cock a deaf 'un'. Supermen don't need advice and Supermen most definitely don't heed unwanted advice. The only thing which might conceivably nudge Lester Piggott into even contemplating whether to give up riding racehorses was if there were no racehorses to ride. And that unlikely scenario, in a nutshell, is what had begun to materialise during 1994. Now, even more than ever before, racehorses to Lester Piggott meant racehorses with a better than 50-50 chance of winning; furthermore, the class act wanted class horses. There were sentimentalists and gawkers galore who were ready and willing to put Piggott up on their horses just for the novelty value of being able to relate how they were once in the great man's orbit. But no living legend takes kindly to being made privy to some sort of freak show. A class act, however antiquated, merited class horses. Accordingly, as the number of quality mounts drained away so did Lester Piggott's desire to carry on.

In the first two full seasons of the comeback, 1991 and 1992, the number of horses Piggott partnered in Britain was virtually identical – 322 and 329 – albeit the number of winners dropped from 48 (14.9 per cent) to 35 (10.6 per cent). Boosting these figures, of course, were winners in abundance throughout Europe. Many of these came on decent animals in Pattern races; a total of 14 in each of 1991 (including two Group Is) and 1992 (eight Group Is), for example, stood parity with any of the top jockeys. However, although 1993's 39 British winners actually denoted an upswing in Piggott's winning percentage (13.1) they came from just 298 opportunities. The missing 30-odd rides could easily be explained away:

Susan Piggott's contribution of 60-plus had been halved. More disturbing was the decrease in the number of quality Pattern races to nine: Chapel Cottage's sprint hat-rick (Greenlands; Cork & Orrery; Prix Maurice de Gheest); Danse Royale in the Prix de Pysche; Swing Low in the Lockinge; and a brace apiece from Lord Carnarvon's two fillies – Niche, who won the Nell Gwyn and Falmouth at Newmarket, and Lemon Souffle, who also scored at Newmarket in the Cherry Hinton prior to collecting Piggott's solitary Group I of the season, the Moyglare Stud Stakes at the Curragh. Both quantity and quality continued to slide in 1994: 19 wins from 205 rides (9.3 per cent) and only five Pattern races viz the Falmouth (Lemon Souffle); Greenlands (College Chapel); Gallinule (Right Win); Desmond (Bin Ajwaad) and Premio Ellington (Captain Horatius).

All the signs indicated trainers were becoming increasingly reluctant to put Piggott up on their top horses in the top races. According to John Whiteley's Computer Racing Form, Piggott was only the 44th most effective jockey in Britain, 2.3lb below the average; in the *Independent*, Richard Edmondson quoted one anonymous Newmarket trainer as saying: 'There is no great buzz about in the town anymore because, to be honest, I don't think anyone gives a monkey's! It's only Joe Public outside Newmarket, who still think he's God, who seem to care any more'; was Lester nowadays more passenger than pilot, asked Paul Haigh in the *Post*. Were those

Niche plays her part in the British swansong with a comfortable victory in the 1993 Falmouth Stakes at Newmarket *(Trevor Jones)*

legs of steel wobbling at last; was that rod or iron, once the most fearsome whipping action in the business, finally weakening?

The number of individual trainers who provided Piggott with mounts in Britain between 1991 and 1994 dropped from 85 to 74,70, and finally 58. Significantly, beyond his immediate family circle of wife, brother-in-law and son-in-law, only ten trainers ever gave him ten or more rides in a season during the Second Coming. His principal British benefactor other than Susan Piggott (181 rides) was Richard Hannon (117). Indeed, Hannon and Susan Piggott accounted for 1 in 4 of Lester's 1154 British rides and 1 in 3 of the 141 successes. With the declining input of Susan Piggott (quantity) and Vincent O'Brien (quality) Piggott's fortunes in 1993 and 1994 in particular would have been lean to the point of emaciation without Richard Hannon who provided nearly 40 per cent (19 of the 58) of the British winners that were highlighted by Right Win, Swing Low, Niche and Lemon Souffle on the vital Pattern-race front.

Unfortunately for Piggott, Niche and Lemon Souffle, his two best mounts during 1993 and 1994, were both prevented by misfortune from improving this bleak outlook. Niche was killed in an accident with a van after breaking loose on Richard Hannon's gallops in August 1993; in addition to that year's Nell Gwyn and Falmouth she and Piggott had come second in the 1,000 Guineas, while the previous season they won the Group III Queen Mary Stakes at Royal Ascot and the Group II Lowther Stakes at York.

The year younger Lemon Souffle ran up a sequence of four victories in Piggott's hands, which included the Group III Cherry Hinton Stakes and Group I Moyglare Stud Stakes, before she sustained a badly gashed hind leg when finishing third in the Cheveley Park Stakes at Newmarket in October. The injury appeared career-threatening. Lemon Souffle missed the 1994 1,000 Guineas but Hannon's vets repaired the tendon with skin grafts taken from the filly's stomach. A promising reappearance at Royal Ascot in June set her up nicely for a tilt at the Falmouth Stakes, which she duly won. 'This was a win Piggott needed badly, his season until yesterday having been something of a flop', commented Richard Griffiths in his *Racing Post* report. It was his 289th and final victory in a British Pattern race (raising the European total to 465 overall). Sadly, it was three months before Lemon Souffle ran again and then it was only to disappoint; she was subsequently retired. The pragmatic owner of Niche and Lemon Souffle had no qualms about the ability of their jockey. 'He's just as good as he has ever been in the big races', said Lord Carnarvon, 'and I wouldn't agree at all with comments that he is not as strong as ever.'

In many respects, the Newmarket July Meeting of 1993 was Piggott's British swansong. On the Tuesday Lemon Souffle won the Cherry Hinton; on Wednesday Niche added the Falmouth; and on the Thursday Piggott won the competitive Bunbury Cup on En Attendant. 'He is a very hard ride', said the horse's trainer Ben Hanbury. 'He hangs both ways and puts his head in the air. But he and Lester get on very well together. Lester told me: 'I'm good with the difficult ones'.

Peter O'Sullevan was in no doubt where the reasons for Piggott's dwindling fortunes lay: 'I think Lester is being more selective in his rides. He is acutely aware of the fact that if he rides moderate horses and ends up on a succession of losers it will inhibit his prospects of getting better rides. Obviously, he'd like to get more significant rides but it's difficult because most of the top stables have their own riders. The number of spare rides of quality are very limited indeed. I would say he is practically as good as ever. Obviously, he can't be quite as good as he was; it's inevitable that he has lost some of his strength but riding is not about physical strength, it's about fitness and skills. I don't think his jockeyship is any weaker, he's as brilliant a tactician as he ever was and I don't think there are any physical demands that he can't match up to. Asking when he's going to stop riding is like asking when I'll give up commentating! I don't know. I think both of us will stop when we feel we're not doing it properly any more.'

Piggott's response to all this incessant tittle-tattle was suitably pithy. 'In my life in racing I have gone my own way and it will be like that until I finish', he told the *Daily Express*; to *The Mail on Sunday* he was slightly more expansive: 'Of course, things are not the same any more. There are not the glut of mounts there used to be. The telephone doesn't ring so constantly. But that is perfectly understandable...the horses are not just there for me any more. Most of the top stables and leading owners have their own retained riders and the competition among jockeys is fierce. It is not that easy to pick up rides, especially on good horses. I feel terrific and in excellent shape. I still enjoy riding. I get a tremendous thrill from it and as long as it continues to give me pleasure I'll keep doing it.' Toward the end of the 1994 Turf season he added: 'I shall be celebrating my 59th birthday in the best way possible – in the saddle. Unless anything unforseen happens it is also the way I intend to celebrate by 60th birthday a year from now. I fully intend to make myself available to any trainer who would like to engage my services next season.' Mr Confusion was Lester's 59th birthday mount in Doncaster's November Handicap which traditionally winds up the Flat season; they came 21st.

Despite those birthday resolutions the news that Piggott was delaying his return to Britain in the spring of 1995 in favour of extending his working holiday in Australia set the tongues wagging again. By the time Piggott was expected back the Classics would be underway and any plum 'spares' already snapped up. Then, when he did return in April, he declined to apply for a new domestic licence; and he was also writing his autobiography for publication in the autumn to coincide with his 60th birthday on November 5th. The message was as plain as a pikestaff: who would be the first to break the story?

On May 3rd, John de Moraville announced 'Piggott Quits!' in the *Daily Express*. Oh no he hasn't, replied Susan Piggott and Robert Armstrong in the *Racing Post*, he is merely resting after a busy winter abroad. This 'story', they insisted, 'looks like a circulation stunt.' But if Piggott did ride where would the necessary ammunition come from? There would be no help from Vincent O'Brien any more; Peter Chapple- Hyam had not used him since Rodrigo de Triano's campaign two seasons ago. Of the major yards Richard Hannon and Jack Berry pledged their support, as did former weighing room colleague Geoff Lewis. 'I wouldn't have to think twice about putting him on a good horse ... but he'd be the first to admit that he wouldn't want to ride a horse that needs to be scrubbed along for two miles. On a good horse he's still better than 75 per cent of jockeys.'

Lewis had hit the nail bang on the head. The supply of 'good horses' was the key. And that supply had dried up. 'He could manipulate rides like nobody else', recalled Willie Carson. 'That was one of his great strengths. If the trainer didn't want him on a horse, he'd go to the owner. He was quite ruthless in that way. But he can't get away with half of what he used to in the old days. Things have changed dramatically.'

Although Piggott had not applied for a British licence he could – he maintained – have still ridden in the Derby using his Australian licence which did not expire until June 30th. He had not forsaken all hope of finding that elusive tenth Derby winner; he even underwent a secret medical to prove his fitness. 'I certainly have not made any decision to stop riding. I had a very busy winter in Australia, the Far East and Dubai, and I came home ready for a rest and I am still relaxing. But physically I am as good as ever. I ride out two or three mornings a week and I could get the leg up on a horse tomorrow if I felt it was the right opportunity for me. I appreciate the public would like to know what my plans are but the truth is that I have an open mind on the matter. I have to be realistic and say that this will be my last chance to ride in the Derby. Time catches up with everybody. It would be unlikely that I would still be riding next year.

But all the riding arrangements have been sorted out and you wouldn't want anything to go wrong to spoil them.' Piggott's telephone stayed silent; 20 years ago he would have been using it to check those 'arrangements' and, possibly, even go so far as to 'spoil' them.

When Piggott's name failed to appear alongside any of the 15 runners on June 10th the end at last seemed nigh. The previous summer Piggott's 36th ride in the Derby (a total second only to the 38 of Victorian jockey John Osborne, who won just the once) had been Khamaseen, a 33–1 outsider from John Dunlop's yard. Demonstrating exactly why Vincent O'Brien considered him worth 7lb round Epsom, Lester steered Khamaseen through a rough race to finish fifth of the 25 to Dunlop's first string, Erhaab. It was Khamaseen's best form of the season; Piggott's 166th and final ride in an English Classic. Twelve months later, as Lammtarra and Walter Swinburn stole the headlines, the greatest Derby jockey of them all was hosting a picnic in the new Paddock Pavilion as a guest of the race sponsor, Vodafone.

It was now widely acknowledged that English racegoers had seen the last of Lester Keith Piggott. But there was still the lure of one more lucrative and sentimental swansong in the Far East. 'Lester wouldn't tell his left hand what his right hand was doing', said Geoff Lewis in August, 'but I got the impression he's just freshening himself up for a winter tour overseas.' Another former colleague in Jimmy Lindley concurred: 'It wouldn't surprise me if he didn't ride here again because I know Lester doesn't want to be going round the back on bad horses but he's still a very big name out in the Far East, a living legend if you like. He did extremely well in Australia and other places over the last winter and I think the style of racing abroad, where horses do it a lot more on the bridle, suits the older rider. Lester's brain is still needle sharp but the old bones do get weaker and when it comes to a slugging match you can't lay up with an 18 year old. Lester gets better horses, comparatively, to ride when he travels; he brings people to the track. He's still a great name to put forward.' However, it was Lewis who once more struck precisely the right chord: 'Lester is a freak, a genius, but I do hope he gives up racing before it gives up on him.'

Official confirmation that Lester Piggott had indeed decided to 'give up' racing came on Sunday, September 10th:'I've had offers to ride again but when you've got a problem with your weight it's just no fun. I've found it difficult to motivate myself and get the weight off this year. I've had a lot of pleasure from my riding but I've had enough now. I'm tired of struggling to keep my weight down. I've had a long career and could have gone on. But eventually you don't want to do it any more even though you know how much you will miss it. Part of me wanted to stay involved in racing on the domestic scene but another part of me just couldn't be bothered. I have always thought that if you don't want to do something wholeheartedly you shouldn't do it at all. So I didn't.'

Thus, Mr Confusion went down in the history books as the 21,002nd and the last horse to be assisted by Lester Piggott on the Flat in Britain; the last of the 4493 winners was Palacegate Jack at Haydock Park – the same location as the first 46 years earlier – on October 5th, 1994.

The obituary notices and tributes could fill a book in their own right. 'It's Over', declared the *Racing Post*. The paper's editorial director Brough Scott expressed his thoughts in a piece entitled: 'The warrior whom we should never forget'. At the heart of the tribute Scott wrote: 'And now only the legend lives on. That's as it should be. For now we can give the legend its due. In a very real sense he was a freak, a genius and not surprisingly sometimes an awkward cuss to boot. The friction in his personality was an essential part of his greatness.' The racing industry's other organ broke the news with 'Piggott bows out'. Its editorial was headed: 'Hail and Farewell' and concluded with the lines: 'Piggott was unique. He was no London bus. There will not be another along in a minute. Indeed not ever.' These sentiments found echoes throughout 'Fleet Street'.

'Greatest Show on Turf' (*Daily Star*) 'Bye, Bye Lester' (*Daily Mirror*) 'Lester Day's Man' (*The Sun*) 'Time overtakes peerless Piggott' (*Daily Mail*) 'Lester finally takes weight off his mind' (*Daily Telegraph*) 'Piggott calls time on a glorious career' (*The Times*)

Current champion Frankie Dettori led the parade of champion jockeys who paid homage to the Old Master:

Frankie Dettori: 'The name speaks for itself. He was the greatest. I had heard about Lester as a young boy in Italy and although I didn't see him right at his peak he was still very special and a great guy to have around. He had nerves of steel. I was on Markofdistinction when he won the Breeders' Cup Mile on Royal Academy. That was some ride!'

Willie Carson: 'He had a great will to win and he was a very hard man to beat. He was always unpredictable but he got himself on the best horses. He revolutionised riding styles as he rode very short because he was on the tall side for a jockey. Because of that you could always pick out the Piggott silhouette with the bottom sticking up in the air, and you knew the longer it stayed that way the better he was going. There have been two great jockeys in the 20th century – Gordon Richards and Lester Piggott – and although there will be other great jockeys there will not be another Lester.'

Pat Eddery: 'I thought Lester would carry on and was looking forward to several more of our famous battles. He was a great ambassador for our sport.'

Michael Roberts: 'I got to know Lester through my early days with Fred Rickaby in South Africa. I was always fascinated by Lester and Mr Rickaby had all the books about him. I tried to copy Lester's style, though not riding so short because it felt uncomfortable. Then Lester started coming out to South Africa and I watched him and got to know him. He could win races with all sorts of tactics. He'd win from the front, he'd come from behind – he'd come from anywhere! I remember him winning this fillies' Guineas back home on Dark Elf. First he was on the outside of five horses as we approached the turn and the next moment he was on the rails! This filly usually pulled but Lester was riding her on a long rein and had her so relaxed that he slowed the pace to half-speed and had us racing outside him. Just as I thought she must be tiring Lester shook Dark Elf up and they shot forward to catch the rest of us completely napping. He was the best I've ever seen, the best I'm ever likely to see and I have the utmost respect and admiration for him.'

Joe Mercer: 'There has never been a better jockey – he was brilliant in his day and has had a tremendous career. He has done so much for British racing – he was the first one to start riding abroad. Let him enjoy a life and have some fun. I hear he's playing golf. Everything he does is unorthodox so I don't suppose his golf will be any different! I'm hoping to get a game with him.'

Steve Cauthen: 'Lester was one of the greatest. I always had the utmost admiration for him and to me his riding comeback was the equivalent of Sugar Ray Leonard returning after five years out of the ring. It was such an athletic feat. I know how fit you have to be to ride. He was off for five years and yet he still came back. There is always a time to hang it up. But racing was Lester's life and he couldn't find anything to take its place. He had to go back. I'm sure that he wasn't as physically strong at the end but he was mentally tough. He was always a very tough competitor. He would always do the unexpected. And he was very cool. He would ride the Derby like it was a claiming race, he was so calm and collected.'

Bill Shoemaker: 'I'm sorry to hear that he's hanging it up. He was a lot like me...we both had longevity. I have all the respect in the world for him. He was certainly one of the best ever. He was very strong and he had a great head for riding. He got more out of a horse than 99 per cent of other riders could.'

Mick Kinane: 'Really, there is only one thing you can say about Lester Piggott – he was the best. I remember watching him win the Derby on The Minstrel when I was an apprentice and it was unbelievable. He'd probably get a six-month suspension for it in this day and age, but I thought it was one of the best rides ever.'

Christy Roche: 'It's nice that he has retired when he's ready and not because of media pressure or whatever. He was the greatest, no question. He broke all the old traditions and gave jockeys a status they didn't have previously. He carved out a new generation of jockeys with his style and ability. I know he would jock off some of us on occasion but it was almost accepted that this happened with Lester.'

Yves Saint-Martin: 'He was my principal adversary all my life. I had terrific admiration and respect for him. Lester was one of the greatest jockeys the world has ever known.'

Freddie Head: 'He's a man who made history. A legend.'

Walter Swinburn proved an eloquent spokesman for all those practitioners unable to call themselves a champion and included in his valediction a story which said so much about Piggott's longevity: 'When I came from Ireland he took me under his wing. I used to stay with him and learned from his great discipline. He would lock away his Yorkie bars and cigars. When he unlocked the cupboard he would take out one piece of chocolate at a time. There will never be a jockey like him again. I was in awe of the man, he was genius.'

Assessments from the many trainers and owners who had cause to thank Piggott were led by Vincent O'Brien:

Vincent O'Brien: 'When you talk of Lester Piggott you must talk in superlatives. To me, he was a genius. Lester was a brilliant jockey – he had no equal. He was a great strategist. He would analyse races both before and

98

afterwards. He had great empathy with his horses. He was a brave jockey and had nerves of steel. In short, he was a born professional. When you look back on his career in years to come, we will realise that he is incomparable. Lester Piggott is a man apart.'

Henry Cecil: 'Lester's retirement marks the end of an era and he's probably one of the greatest jockeys of all time. He has been brilliant on so many occasions and he will leave a gap that will take an awfully long time to fill.'

Tom Jones: 'He rode my first Classic winner, Athens Wood, and it was a typical Lester ride. He waited in front while everyone behind him thought they would be able to come and do him, but he kept that little bit up his sleeve and won by a neck. One never quite knew what to expect from Lester, but he was a great man to have on your side.'

Maurice Zilber: 'It's the end of a fascinating era. I was lucky to have Lester as a jockey, for Empery in the Derby and for Dahlia. He was the greatest of all. I think he still owes me £100! Some time ago at Longchamp a lady lost a bet with me after I said my horse would finish in front of hers. I saw her a few weeks later and asked her for the money. She told me it had been given to Lester, who I suppose still has it!'

Peter Chapple-Hyam: 'He was the greatest and has done more for racing than any other single person. It made me chuckle to think he won the 2,000 Guineas for me when he had ridden a Derby winner before I was born! Lester's been everyone's idol, hasn't he? It's sad that we won't see him race again but we have to be pleased he has got out in one piece. He was the best there has ever been.'

Dick Hern: 'What can one say – he's a man who was a legend in his own lifetime and I don't suppose we who lived through his career will ever see anyone to match his record.'

Robert Sangster: 'I think Lester is the greatest jockey of this century and the previous century as well. The crowd love him and that's what it's all about. This is an entertainment business and Lester is the best in the business.'

Lord Carnarvon: 'Lester was and still is a character. Alongside Gordon Richards, I would rate him the best jockey I have seen – and I was fortunate enough to see Steve Donoghue and all the great Australians. Gordon perhaps lost fewer races that he should have won than Lester but, against that, Lester had that rare spark of genius.'

Then there were the privileged onlookers:

Peter O'Sullevan: 'One of the extraordinary aspects of Lester's career was the fact that he nearly always managed to get himself on the best horses. He had very little consideration for the feelings of his colleagues but it was to their eternal credit that they accepted the fact that he was superior. They idolised him on account of his talent.'

John Oaksey: 'It's sad in one way but not sad at all in another. As far as I am concerned he never deteriorated – he's going out at the top with dignity. It will make Flat racing duller. All my life in racing the most exciting thing you watched in Flat racing was Lester Piggott.'

John McCririck: 'I'm delighted – it was an overdue decision. The professional trainers simply weren't putting him up. Lester's bottle may not have gone but it's a young man's sport and we would all have been guilty if any serious injury had happened.'

Louis Romanet: 'He traversed a generation and I remember him when I was a little boy. He was an amazing personality and a real figurehead. He showed such courage when falling on Mr Brooks at the Breeders' Cup. I was the stewards' secretary when he borrowed Alain Lequeux's whip in the Grand Prix de Deauville. He had the stewards in laughter when he told them that Lequeux had offered it to him after he dropped his own.'

Jeffrey Bernard: 'We have been gradually getting used to the idea of Lester Piggott retiring from racing and yet he keeps reappearing for us to glimpse at him. But this latest announcement has the ring of finality. I am still trying to get used to the idea but no Piggott is going to be like eggs without bacon. Royal Ascot, for example, will be a banquet without any flavour. I miss him already, although he is still with us, and the daily lists of runners and riders in the newspapers seem strangely lacking without his name. Racing is now almost Marks without Spencer. It is going to be an extremely hard, if not impossible, act to follow and it must be odd for him to reflect that he was, in his time, the best in the world at what he did. I feel almost lucky to have met the man and to know him even slightly...and a photograph of the two of us together takes pride of place on the wall of my study.'

Lastly, that body of men glad to see the back of him – the bookmakers:

Mike Dillon: 'He scared all us bookmakers to death and over the years has cost us millions. But he raised the whole profile of the sport when it started appearing live on TV and with the advent of betting shops. He was always the housewive's choice, especially in the Derby. It was simple – when Piggott won, we lost!'

Members of the public made their opinion known by ringing the Cabinet Office to recommend a knighthood, an initiative in keeping with John Major's recent call for such nominations. 'There are an awful lot of people who have made a much smaller contribution to our national life and been knighted', observed Maureen Piggott. Willie Carson added his support: 'The best gesture would be if the Queen gave him a knighthood. Everybody in racing would share my view – he deserves it. Personally I'd love to see it, but I just don't think it will happen. I don't see how the powers-that-be would allow it.'

In *The Mail on Sunday*, Patrick Collins was equally pragmatic: 'Had things been different, then he would certainly have been knighted in the twilight years of his career. Sadly, the prison sentence ensured that the sword would never descend upon his shoulder, but his dearest wish is that some way be found to restore his OBE. There surely would be no great surge of disapproval if simple justice should usurp stale custom, and certainly there would be no objection from a racing monarch who has been present at so many of Piggott's triumphs.'

The *Racing Post*, nevertheless, went so far as to put the matter of a possible knighthood to a Cabinet Office spokesperson who was quoted as saying: 'Just because somebody has been in prison and served their time would not necessarily mean their name could not be processed for an award. His case is different in that he has already received an OBE which was removed. That is a complication which I don't think we have ever found before. We are working on the New Year's List at the moment. In theory it is a bit late but in a case like this when we have just heard that he has retired we can always consider it.' Piggott, as down to earth as ever, confided himself to saying: 'It's not something that can ever happen, is it?'

Lester was right; as was William Hill who had offered odds of 50–1 against such an eventuality. There was, however, no likelihood of Piggott being forgotten by the sport he had graced and served so well for nigh on half a century. In December 1995, the Horserace Writers' Association presented him with the George Ennor Trophy for Outstanding Achievement. At long last even the BBC got in on the act. Despite Piggott's massive catalogue of achievement in a sport boasting an avid and more fervent following than most, BBC viewers had somehow persistently ignored Lester's genuine claims to the Sports Personality of the Year award whilst freely bestowing it upon sundry others, including some less deserving equestrians. With, no doubt, a few subtle promptings from Peter O'Sullevan, the BBC consequently decided to mint a Special Award for Services to the Sport of Racing which the doyen of racing commentators handed over during the Sports Review of the Year programme on Sunday, December 10th. O'Sullevan's presentation speech was a model of tact and diplomacy: 'Lester, I have to admit, that annually for 41 years I have expected your unique talent to be recognised by BBC TV Sport. I'm rather sad that it's so belated but I'm very proud and very honoured to present you with this unique trophy which is in recognition of your utterly unique talent.' Three months later, the 1996 'Lesters' joined in by including a lengthy visual tribute played out to a cacophony of clapping, cheering and singing along to Tina Turner's most appropriate of anthems.

However, although Lester's status as 'Simply the Best' may be assured within the world of racing, he was considered far from 'The Greatest' in a Channel 4 series of that name which appraised the merits of an elite group of 20 British sportsmen and sportswomen. The complex scoring process involved marks out of 20 in five categories viz achievement, dominance, style (including sportsmanship), fortitude (notably self-discipline and the will-to-win) and impact. Lester's case was made courtesy of a filmed insert narrated by Hugh McIlvanney and supported by a studio contribution from John Francome. The former champion National Hunt jockey awarded Piggott a very high score of 90 but the all-important studio audience and phone-in marks which would decide the issue, resulted in an average of just 69, ahead of such luminaries as Steve Ovett, Bobby Moore and Jackie Stewart but only enough for 13th place some way behind the eventual winner Daley Tompson on 81.

At the same time (April 1996) Epsom racecourse announced that the gates next to the Queen's Stand were to be named in Piggott's honour. Epsom's director of racing Edward Gillespie explained: 'When Lester retired we felt it was incredibly important that he should have a perpetual tribute at Epsom because his impact on the racecourse and the Derby has

'Simply the Best': Lester gets to grips with one of his metallic alter egos *(Trevor Jones)*

been longer and more dominant than any other sportsman at any other venue: his name will always be inextricably linked with the Derby.'

Thus did Lester Piggott join the hallowed company of two other sporting icons, W G Grace and Bill Shankly, who are immortalised by gates at Lord's and Anfield respectively. Mounted on the gates will be reproductions of specially commissioned paintings by Roy Miller depicting Piggott's nine Derby wins, six Oaks and nine Coronation Cups, plus a written tribute from Peter O'Sullevan that said: 'It was Epsom, the world's most varied and demanding Grade 1 racecourse, that became his supreme arena. No jockey has exercised a greater hold on the imagination of the sporting public. Annually, as the month of June approached, the cardinal question was. 'What will Lester ride in the Derby?'

Every horse and rider will pass through the Piggott Gates when they walk from the paddock on to the course. 'I hope they don't fall off when they see me up there', quipped Lester. More seriously, he added: 'When I heard about the idea I was absolutely delighted. The history and tradition of the Derby make it very special and totally unique in the world of racing. The Derby was always very special to me and to be honoured in this way is a great thrill. It is a wonderful tribute and the paintings are terrific. I couldn't ask for anything more.'

The Second Coming of Lester Piggott had seen 'The Galloping Grandfather' and 'The Great Antiquity' added to the litany of well-worn epithets which numbered 'The Long Fella', 'Old Stoneface' and 'A Face Like a Well-Kept Grave'. Terms of endearment, each and every one, which sub-editors could now put away for good. How will posterity attempt to sum up Lester Keith Piggott? Churchill once described Russia as 'a riddle wrapped in a mystery inside an enigma.' That just about describes Piggott the man. And as a jockey? Susan Piggott best identified the reason for her husband's elite position in racing's hall of fame when she once said of him: 'He's as close to being a centaur as any man can be.'

Appendix One

BRITISH WINS

1990

16 October	Chepstow	Nicholas 6–4 on fav
		Biddestone All-Aged Stakes (Susan Piggott)
"	"	Shining Jewel 11–1
		Gainsborough Claiming Stakes (Eric Eldin)
19 October	Newmarket	Chimayo 9–1
		Snailwell Maiden Stakes (Barry Hills)

TOTAL: 3 wins; 4 seconds; 3 thirds from 39 rides

1991

23 March	Lingfield	La Masaas 11–8on fav
		Mosquito Claiming Stakes (Pat Haslam)
"	"	First Stage 7–2
		Wellington Claiming Stakes (Ian Campbell)
25 March	Folkestone	Rare Detail 3–1 fav
		Kingsworth Handicap (Susan Piggott)
15 April	Folkestone	Shafouri 7–2
		Chatham Maiden Stakes (Susan Piggott)
18 April	Newmarket	Golan Heights 6–1
		Remy Martin VSOP Cognac Handicap
		(Julie Cecil)
"	"	Nicholas 9–4 fav
		Boadicea Handicap (Susan Piggott)
20 April	Newbury	St Ninian 100–30 fav
		Spring Cup (Mick Easterby)
"	"	BOG TROTTER 4–1
		G3 GREENHAM STAKES, £22,134
		(William Haggas)

2 May	Newmarket	Saddler's Hall 7–4 fav Hintlesham Hall May Stakes (Michael Stoute)
6 May	Kempton	St Ninian 9–4 fav Jubilee Handicap, (Mick Easterby)
"	"	El Yasaf 13–2 Appledore Handicap (Bill Stubbs)
17 May	Newbury	POLAR FALCON 3–1 G2 LOCKINGE STAKES, £40,902 (John Hammond)
20 May	Folkestone	Bit-A-Magic 13–8on fav Metropole Challenge Cup (Jack Berry)
"	"	Sizzling Saga 6–4 fav Glover Insurance Stakes (Jack Berry)
27 May	Sandown	Busted Rock 15–8 fav UB Coating Handicap (Susan Piggott)
28 May	Leicester	Master of Passion 6–4 fav Woodhouse Eaves Maiden Stakes (James Eustace)
31 May	Nottingham	Huso 8–1 Eastwood Handicap (Pat Haslam)
4 June	Yarmouth	Sought Out 6–4on fav Blackfriars Maiden Stakes (Michael Stoute)
6 June	Epsom	Burdur 10–1 Nightingall Maiden Stakes (Ben Hanbury)
7 June	Epsom	Green Dollar 9–1 Tokyo Trophy Handicap (Eric Wheeler)
18 June	Royal Ascot	SADDLER'S HALL 7–1 G2 KING EDWARD VII STAKES, £56,673 (Michael Stoute)
3 July	Warwick	Beau Quest 14–1 Syd Mercer Memorial Trophy (Richard Woodhouse)
4 July	Yarmouth	Busted Rock 3–1 fav J Medler Ltd Handicap (Susan Piggott)
16 July	Leicester	Mamma's Too 11–10on fav Radio Leicester Nursery (Jack Berry)
"	"	Affordable 15–2 Cardinal Wolsey Handicap (Willie Carson)

16 July	Leicester	Micheletti 13–8on fav Glebe Maiden Stakes (Henry Cecil)
24 July	Sandown	Ninja Dancer 5–1 Capital Gold Maiden (Julie Cecil)
25 July	Yarmouth	Masai Mara 5–1 Belton Handicap (Pat Haslam)
1 August	Goodwood	Itsagame 20–1 Citroen ZX Handicap (Simon Dow)
2 August	Newmarket	Micheletti 13–8on fav Running Gap Stakes (Henry Cecil)
3 August	Windsor	Aedean 5–2 fav Molson Special Dry Maiden (Charles Elsey)
7 August	Pontefract	Threshfield 11–10on fav Jim Gundill Memorial Handicap (Barney Curley)
19 August	Windsor	Fivesevenfiveo 7–4 fav Belmead Selling Stakes (Jack Berry)
"	"	Surrealist 11–10on fav Theale Graduation Stakes (Barry Hills)
20 August	York	Micheletti 11–2 Melrose Handicap (Henry Cecil)
23 August	Goodwood	Burdur 7–1 Schroder Investments Management Handicap (Ben Hanbury)
5 September	Salisbury	Basma 7–2 Dick Poole Stakes (Dick Hern)
"	"	Balasani 11–4 fav Salisbury Festival Handicap (Martin Pipe)
10 September	Leicester	Songster 4–1 fav Tattersalls Maiden (Jimmy Fitzgerald)
12 September	Leicester	BOG TROTTER 11–2 G3 KIVETON PARK STAKES, £24,435 (William Haggas)
"	"	Mudaffar 16–1 People-Sporting Life Handicap (Robert Armstrong)
14 September	Doncaster	You Know The Rules 14–1 Sceptre Stakes (Mick Channon)

17 September	Yarmouth	Shining Jewel 4–1 J Medler Ltd Handicap (Eric Eldin)
23 September	Nottingham	Lord Oberon 3–1 jt fav Carlton Claiming Stakes (Ben Hanbury)
1 October	Newcastle	Able Quest 6–5 fav Polworth Maiden (Robert Armstrong)
10 October	Yarmouth	Fylde Flyer 13–2 Tetley Bitter Nursery (Jack Berry)
14 October	Leicester	Claret 5–4on fav Badger Stakes (Dick Hern)

TOTAL: 48 wins; 42 seconds; 44 thirds from 322 rides

1992

14 April	Newmarket	Fylde Flyer 9–1 (L) Abernant Stakes (Jack Berry)
2 May	Newmarket	RODRIGO DE TRIANO 6–1 G1 2000 GUINEAS, £113,736 (Peter Chapple-Hyam)
9 May	Lingfield	Flight Lieutenant 9–4 Turnell Chilled Distribution Maiden (Philip Mitchell)
15 May	Newmarket	Niche 13–8 fav Ditch Fillies Median Auction Stakes (Richard Hannon)
"	"	King Olaf 15–8 fav King Charles II Stakes (Peter Chapple-Hyam)
23 May	Haydock	Jervia 7–1 St Helens Maiden Fillies (Bill Watts)
25 May	Redcar	Thamestar 2–1 on fav Billingham Maiden (John Dunlop)
2 June	Folkestone	Liffey River 11–4 fav Sellinage Selling Stakes (Susan Piggott)
"	"	Snow Blizzard 10–1 Crown Inn Rye Handicap (Simon Dow)
13 June	York	Ringland 8–1 Macmillan Nurse Appeal Handicap (Pat Haslam)
18 June	Royal Ascot	NICHE 9–1 G3 NORFOLK STAKES, £22,707 (Richard Hannon)

26 June	Doncaster	Hadeer's Dancer 7–4 fav Margaret Maiden Auction (Robert Armstrong)
30 June	Folkestone	Snow Blizzard 15–8 fav Disk Maker Challenge Cup (Simon Dow)
1 July	Yarmouth	Inseyab 5–2 jt fav Fastolff Selling Stakes (Pat Haslam)
"	"	Shining Jewel 5–2 fav South Walsham Handicap (Susan Piggott)
4 July	Haydock	Love of Silver 6–4on fav July Maiden (Clive Brittain)
6 July	Windsor	Bold Boss 9–4 fav National Association of Boys Clubs Handicap (Ben Hanbury)
9 July	Newmarket	MR BROOKS 16–1 G1 JULY CUP, £92,619 (Richard Hannon)
15 July	Yarmouth	Miss Fayruz 5–4 fav Harrison Selling Stakes (Susan Piggott)
4 August	Brighton	Troon 6–4 fav Alfriston Maiden (Susan Piggott)
5 August	Brighton	Liffey River 10–1 Levy Board Handicap (Susan Piggott)
11 August	Yarmouth	Shining Jewel 11–4 Levy Board Handicap (Susan Piggott)
18 August	York	RODRIGO DE TRIANO 8–1 G1 JUDDMONTE INTERNATIONAL, £164,852 (Peter Chapple-Hyam)
20 August	York	NICHE 2–1 G2 LOWTHER STAKES, £88,502 (Richard Hannon)
28 August	Goodwood	Jahangir 7–1 Schroder Investments Management Handicap (Ben Hanbury)
2 September	York	Never So Sure 6–1 fav Lawrence Batley Handicap (Alan Bailey)
5 September	Haydock	Mr Confusion 4–1 Websters Yorkshire Bitter Handicap (Steve Norton)

8 September	Lingfield	Albert the Bold 5–1 Beefeater Gin Handicap (Susan Piggott)
21 September	Folkestone	Rain Brother 2–1 Walmer Stakes (Peter Chapple-Hyam)
22 September	Nottingham	Snowy River 3–1 Colwick Median Auction (Jon Scargill)
"	"	Jumaira Star 2–1 fav Fiskerton Maiden (John Gosden)
17 October	Newmarket	RODRIGO DE TRIANO 11–8 fav G1 CHAMPION STAKES, £216,176 (Peter Chapple-Hyam)
20 October	Chester	Jackpot Star 11–10 fav Saltney Maiden (Richard Hannon)
24 October	Doncaster	Thamestar 10–1 North America Travel Service Handicap (John Dunlop)

TOTAL: 35 wins; 45 seconds; 36 thirds from 329 rides

1993

30 March	Leicester	Sehailah 15–2 Keythorpe Maiden Fillies (Susan Piggott)
12 April	Kempton	Lucky Guest 7–1 Rosebery Stakes (John Dunlop)
13 April	Newmarket	NICHE 11–1 G3 NELL GWYN STAKES, £21,961 (Richard Hannon)
14 April	Newmarket	Pommes Frites 5–4 fav Bartlow Maiden (Richard Hannon)
26 April	Windsor	Lemon Souffle 3–1 Lady Caroline Fillies Stakes (Richard Hannon)
3 May	Kempton	Brockton Dancer 10–1 Shield Club Fillies Stake (Richard Hannon)
"	"	Pay Homage 12–1 Jubilee Handicap (Ian Balding)
"	"	Dramanie 11–4 fav Classic Cars Maiden (Julie Cecil)
6 May	Brighton	Bid For Blue 11–4 fav St Ann's Wells Maiden (Richard Hannon)

6 May	Brighton	Exhibit Air 9–2 Vardean Maiden (Richard Hannon)
10 May	Windsor	Southern Memories 5–1 Piccadilly Handicap (Richard Hannon)
14 May	Newbury	SWING LOW 12–1 G2 LOCKINGE STAKES, £38,898 (Richard Hannon)
17 May	Bath	Desert Lore 3–1 Timeform Card Maiden (Lord Huntingdon)
18 May	Goodwood	Geisway 9–2 (L) Predominate Stakes (Richard Hannon)
26 May	Newbury	Governor George 5–1 Boxford Maiden (Richard Hannon)
10 June	Newbury	Lemon Souffle 5–4 fav Sokkens Masterstroke Stakes (Richard Hannon)
12 June	Nottingham	Monsignor Pat 7–2 Nottingham Evening Post Handicap (Richard Hannon)
17 June	Royal Ascot	COLLEGE CHAPEL 7–2 fav G3 CORK & ORRERY STAKES, £40,645 (Vincent O'Brien)
18 June	Newmarket	En Attendant 7–1 Kidsons Impney Trophy (Ben Hanbury)
22 June	Yarmouth	Golden Guest 3–1 fav Tote Place Only Maiden Fillies (Julie Cecil)
25 June	Newmarket	Call Me I'm Blue 9–4 fav Merivale Moore Handicap (Nigel Tinkler)
"	"	Saihat 11–8on fav Unicite Maiden (Julie Cecil)
28 June	Windsor	Barahin 7–2 Montrose Selling Stakes (Roland O'Sullivan)
1 July	Yarmouth	Shining Jewel evens fav High Steward Claiming Stakes (Susan Piggott)
6 July	Newmarket	LEMON SOUFFLE 5–4on fav G3 CHERRY HINTON STAKES, £15,845 (Richard Hannon)

6 July	Newmarket	NICHE 13–8 fav G2 FALMOUTH STAKES, £38,483 (Richard Hannon)
8 July	Newmarket	En Attendant 14–1 Banbury Cup (Ben Hanbury)
"	Chepstow	Mack The Knife 6–4on fav Welsh Riband Stakes (Dick Hern)
28 July	Goodwood	Call Me I'm Blue 6–1 Charlton Mill Handicap (Nigel Tinkler)
7 August	Lingfield	Jade Pet evens fav South Coast Stakes (Richard Hannon)
11 August	Sandown	Del Deya 14–1 Reid Minty Libel & Slander Maiden (John Gosden)
30 August	Newcastle	Indefence 9–4 fav Rafa Wings Appeal Nursery (Mick Channon)
31 August	Epsom	Never In The Red 11–10on fav Redhill Selling Stakes (Jack Berry)
2 September	Yarmouth	Shining Jewel 11–10on fav Valley Park Claiming Stakes (Susan Piggott)
24 September	Ascot	Call Me I'm Blue 5–1 Army Benevolent Fund Handicap (Nigel Tinkler)
29 September	Newmarket	Fumo di Londra 16–1 Tattersalls Houghton Sales (John Dunlop)
4 October	Warwick	Shoofk 20–1 Vauxhall Master Hire Nursery(Susan Piggott)
18 October	Folkestone	Armenian Coffee 13–2 Hardres Handicap (John Dunlop)
23 October	Doncaster	Ulitmo Imperatore 16–1 F Cross & Sons Doncaster Stakes (John Dunlop)

TOTAL: 39 wins; 27 seconds; 34 thirds from 298 rides

1994

2 May	Kempton	Bold Pursuit 2–1 fav Gold Stakes (Jimmy Fitzgerald)
11 June	Leicester	Mack The Knife 10–1 Leicester Mercury Stakes (Dick Hern)

13 June	Nottingham	Pickles 7–2 fav Test Cricket Handicap (Alan Bailey)
21 June	Newbury	Bin Ajwaad 9–4 fav Avebury Stakes (Ben Hanbury)
22 June	Chester	Futuristic Bent 9–1 Farndon Stakes (Geoff Lewis)
"	"	Pickles 9–2 Deeside Handicap (Alan Bailey)
25 June	Newmarket	With The Fairies 100–30 jt fav Plantation Stud Stakes (Richard Hannon)
6 July	Newmarket	Lemon Souffle 6–5 fav G2 FALMOUTH STAKES, £34,158 (Richard Hannon)
7 July	Newmarket	En Attendant 14–1 Bunbury Cup (Ben Hanbury)
8 July	Chester	Pickles 11–3on fav Harcros Timber & Building Supplies (Alan Bailey)
21 July	Brighton	Possibility 7–2 Raggetts Stakes (Susan Piggott)
22 July	Carlisle	Mazeeka 15–8on fav Stella Artois Claiming Stakes (Mick Channon)
10 August	Sandown	Sergeyev 5–4 fav Squash & Fitness Centre Stakes (Richard Hannon)
16 August	Folkestone	Ansellady 6–4 fav TMP Air Conditioning Stakes (Jack Berry)
25 August	Lingfield	Winners Choice 6–1 Murphy's Irish Stout Stakes (Richard Hannon)
27 August	Goodwood	Strutting 3–1 EBF Solent Stakes (RichardHannon)
7 September	Doncaster	The Jotter 17–2 EBF Carrie Red Nursery (William Jarvis)
28 September	Folkestone	Bahrain Star 5–2 fav Scottish Equitable Stakes (Terry Mills)
5 October	Haydock	Palacegate Jack 9–2 King's Regiment Cup (Jack Berry)

TOTAL: 19 wins; 16 seconds; 23 thirds from 205 rides

Appendix Two

Overseas Wins

(ONLY MAJOR RACES LISTED)

AUSTRALIA: 8

1995	Woodcock Handicap	Caulfield	Swift Encounter
1995	Analie Plate	Randwick	So Keen
1995	Black Opal Prelude	Canberra	Zadok
1995	G2 Black Opal Stakes	Canberra	Zadok

AUSTRIA: 5

1993	Internationale Standard Meile	Freudenau	Lucky Guest
1993	Preis von Casino Linz	Freudenau	New Kid In Town
1993	Preis der Diana	Freudenau	Soft Call

CHILE: 1

FRANCE: 9

1990	Prix le Fabuleux (Listed)	Maisons-Laffitte	Dear Doctor
1992	G1 PRIX DE L'ABBAYE	Longchamp	MR BROOKS
1993	G2 Prix Maurice de Gheest	Deauville	College Chapel
1993	G3 Prix de Pysche	Deauville	Danse Royale
1993	Prix du Pin (Listed)	Longchamp	Sharp Prod

GERMANY: 14

1991	Grosser Tiffany Sprint Preis (Listed)	Munich	Sizzling Saga
1991	G3 Furstenberg Rennen	Baden-Baden	Tao
1991	Preis der Casino (Listed)	Baden-Baden	Glen Flight
1991	G2 Jacobs Goldene Peitsche	Baden-Baden	Nicholas

1991	Preis der Stadt Baden-Baden (Listed)	Baden-Baden	Northern Hal
1991	G2 Moet & Chandon Rennen	Baden-Baden	Showbook
1992	Express Grand Prix Gallop (Listed)	Cologne	Friedland
1992	Gestut Olympis Sprint Cup (Listed)	Krefeld	Canadian Prince
1992	G2 Grosser Preis Von Berlin	Hoppegarten	Mr Brooks
1992	G2 Moet & Chandon Rennen	Baden-Baden	Sharp Prod
1993	Preis der Stadt Baden-Baden (Listed)	Baden-Baden	Lucky Guest
1993	Grosser Silicon Bavaria Sprint Preis (Listed)	Munich	Sharp Prod
1994	Robert Pferdmenges Rennen (Listed)	Hoppegarten	Oenothera

HONG KONG: 6

| 1994 | Hong Kong Classic Trial | Sha Tin | Sterling Town |

INDIA: 4

1991	Indian Turf Invitation Cup	Madras	Delage
1992	Royal Hong Kong Jockey Club Trophy	Bombay	Clark Gable
1995	McDowell Multi Million	Bombay	Nora

IRELAND: 44

1991	Derrinstown Stud 1000 Guineas Trial (Listed)	Leopardstown	Rua D'Oro
1991	G3 Greenlands Stakes	Curragh	Archway
1991	G2 Gallinule Stakes	Curragh	Sportsworld
1991	G3 Railway Stakes	Curragh	El Prado
1991	G1 NATIONAL STAKES	Curragh	EL PRADO
1991	G2 Beresford Stakes	Curragh	El Prado
1991	Goffs Premier Challenge	Curragh	Colway Bold
1992	Leopardstown 2000 Guineas Trial (Listed)	Leopardstown	Portico
1992	G1 2000 GUINEAS	Curragh	RODRIGO DE TRIANO
1992	Brownstown Stud Stakes (Listed)	Leopardstown	Via Borghese

1992 Tyros Stakes (Listed)	Curragh	Fatherland
1992 G3 Futurity Stakes	Curragh	Fatherland
1992 G1 NATIONAL STAKES	Curragh	FATHERLAND
1992 G2 Blandford Stakes	Curragh	Andros Bay
1993 G3 Greenlands Stakes	Curragh	College Chapel
1993 G1 MOYGLARE STUD STAKES	Curragh	LEMON SOUFFLE
1994 G3 Greenlands Stakes	Curragh	College Chapel
1994 G2 Gallinule Stakes	Curragh	Right Win
1994 G3 Desmond Stakes	Curragh	Bin Ajwaad

ITALY: 11

1991 Premio Conte Demanio	Florence	Wild Grouse
1991 Premio Bereguardo (Listed)	San Siro	Wild Grouse
1991 Premio Bimbi (Listed)	San Siro	Bit-A-Magic
1991 G1 GRAN CRITERIUM	San Siro	ALHIJAZ
1992 G1 GRAN PREMIO DEL JOCKEY CLUB E COPPA D'ORO	San Siro	SILVERNESIAN
1994 G2 Premio Ellington	Capannelle	Captain Horatius
1994 Premio Lazio (Listed)	Capannelle	Suplizi

MACAU: 1

SLOVAKIA: 3

1993 Slovenske Derby	Bratislava	Zimzalabim
1993 Bratislava Mile	Bratislava	Laten
1993 Mysa Stakes	Bratislava	Fiorentia

SWEDEN: 1

1991 Svenskt Derby	Jagersro	Tao

TURKEY: 1

1991 G2 Topkapi Trophy	Veliefendi	Lucky Guest

UNITED ARAB EMIRATES: 3 (plus four at a meeting confined to Arab horses)

UNITED STATES: 1

1990 G1 BREEDERS' CUP MILE	Belmont Park	ROYAL ACADEMY